AF610480

Emily Dickinson
Accidental Buddhist

RC Allen

9055 E. Catalina Highway
Apt. 13201
Tucson, AZ 85749

Order this book online at www.trafford.com/06-2155
or email orders@trafford.com

Most Trafford titles are also available at major online book retailers.

Note for Librarians: A cataloguing record for this book is available from Library and Archives Canada at www.collectionscanada.ca/amicus/index-e.html

ISBN: 978-1-4251-0398-9

We at Trafford believe that it is the responsibility of us all, as both individuals and corporations, to make choices that are environmentally and socially sound. You, in turn, are supporting this responsible conduct each time you purchase a Trafford book, or make use of our publishing services. To find out how you are helping, please visit www.trafford.com/responsiblepublishing.html

Our mission is to efficiently provide the world's finest, most comprehensive book publishing service, enabling every author to experience success. To find out how to publish your book, your way, and have it available worldwide, visit us online at www.trafford.com/10510

www.trafford.com

North America & international
toll-free: 1 888 232 4444 (USA & Canada)
phone: 250 383 6864 ♦ fax: 250 383 6804 ♦ email: info@trafford.com

The United Kingdom & Europe
phone: +44 (0)1865 722 113 ♦ local rate: 0845 230 9601
facsimile: +44 (0)1865 722 868 ♦ email: info.uk@trafford.com

10 9 8 7 6 5

ALSO BY RC ALLEN

The Symbolic World of Federico García Lorca

Psyche and Symbol in the Theater of Federico García Lorca

Symbolic Experience: A Study of Poems by Pedro Salinas

The Yin–Yang Journal: An Alternative Reading of the Tao Te Ching

The Yang–Yin Journal: A Critique of the Social Ego

Ambidextrous: A Book of Poems

Solitary Prowess: The Transcendentalist Poetry of Emily Dickinson

TO LINDA

ACCIDENTAL HOTEI

When buddhas don't appear
And their followers are gone,
The wisdom of awakening
Bursts forth by itself.

--Nagarjuna

CONTENTS

PREFACE

This book is self-contained & independent of any previous commentary; at the same time it is a kind of sequel to my earlier study, ***Solitary Prowess: The Transcendentalist Poetry of Emily Dickinson,*** part of an ongoing immersion in the poetry of ED, the Buddha of Amherst. Like ***Solitary Prowess,*** this book consists of a series of close readings of transcendentalist poems by ED.

This format meets a need unrecognized in Dickinson criticism. All the usual Dickinson books deal in generalities about the possible relationship between her poems & her private life. Professor Wolff's tome, ***Emily Dickinson,*** includes some close readings, but they are embedded in discussions of theology and egocentric matters. Conventional readers of ED – including all her commentators – do not even suspect that there is an alternative to egocentric understanding. Buddhist belief & practice, however, are based on the reality of ego-transcendence, the central feature of ED's experience of life, & so it comes as no great surprise that her poetry should dwell on the same archetypal realities.

ED was an amazing wordsmith because she was not limited by the ego-self. Each transcendentalist poem is a special non-ego insight into the dharma, the way things are apart from the ego-reality – their "suchness" (Buddhist *tathata*). ED creates an ad hoc semantics, as does every great poet. This means that the most effective approach to understanding her poems is to examine them one by one, without regard for the private affairs of Emily Dickinson.

In P-501, "This World is not Conclusion," ED wrote that her dharma poetry would "puzzle scholars," as indeed it has. Since mid-twentieth century, scholars have been publishing commentaries on her poetry, all of them egocentric, innocent of any dharma awareness. With the vigorous growth of American Buddhism in the past few decades, however, it is no longer possible to accept or condone academic ignorance of the dharma. Nor is it helpful to categorize ED as a "great American poet," because ED-consciousness transcends the provincial consciousness of Emily Dickinson. She herself comments on this in P-285, "The Robin's my Criterion for Tune," where she says that she speaks "New Englandly" only because she was born in New England. The language of her poetry is contingent upon that – but the dharma of her poetry is not.

The title of my earlier study, ***Solitary Prowess***, refers to P-750, where ED says that "Growth of Man – like Growth of Nature" must achieve its "difficult ideal"

> Through the solitary prowess
> Of a Silent Life –

Any Buddhist engaged in formal meditation recognizes "the solitary prowess of a silent life." ED certainly lived a meditative life, where everyday activities were experienced with a Zen attitude, an identification of mind/matter. Little wonder that gardening was one of her favored activities.

All of the above remarks make clear the title of this second study of ED's poetry, ***Emily Dickinson, Accidental Buddhist***. The Buddha said that anyone who experienced ego-transcendence would experience the Four Noble Truths, just as he did. ED wrote many poems about the Four Noble Truths (as my study shows), not because she knew anything about Buddhism, but because she awoke in the dharma.

FIRST CONSIDERATIONS

AMAZING GRACE

The "wisdom of awakening" is Amazing Grace, church or no church. "Wisdom" means "understanding beyond the limits of ego." The parameters of the ego-self are largely determined by a person's cultural background, but the ego-self is not immutable, & may be altered considerably, both deliberately & accidentally.

Ego-transcendence can produce such an alteration. It can be mild or profound; it can awaken one to a sense of reality far beyond the limits established by the collective ego of one's society.

The highest form of ego-transcendence carries one beyond the limitations of dual thinking (I "in here," the world "out there"), for the transcendent reality is Oneness, or Oceanic Consciousness, where the mind is experienced as an ocean wave, a transient aspect of the ocean itself. There is no substantial self separate from the World Reality.

One's ego-self has been created gradually from childhood, by social conditioning. Ego-transcendence awakens the mind to unconditioned awareness, traditionally called Buddha Mind, Awakened Mind, or the Higher Self.

The wisdom of awakening burst forth by itself in nineteenth-century Amherst, in the person of Emily Dickinson. We like to think of her as a great American poet, but actually there is nothing especially American about her, precisely because Dickinson's Higher Self – ED – is a universal phenomenon unlimited by the boundaries of the ego-self. In P-285 ED says she sees "New Englandly," meaning that she finds her immediate subject matter in the place where she lives; but of course her transcendent subject matter is not determined "New Englandly." Unexpectedly she awakened to the transcendent difference between permanence & impermanence. In a flash she grasped that this was the issue concerning human life, as she observes in P-1257:

> How everlasting are the Lips
> Known only to the Dew –
> These are the Brides of permanence
> Supplanting me and you

The phenomena of Nature are "permanent," in that they recur endlessly, as the Wheel of Life; you & I are "impermanent," not only because we are mortal, but because no ego-self can ever recur, either here or in any afterlife.

ACCIDENTAL BUDDHISM

When enlightenment occurs outside the confines of a theistic religion, a new value system springs into being. It seems inevitable that this would be a kind of "accidental Buddhism," because this is the value system that Gautama Buddha himself discovered. When you do not attempt to adapt ego-transcendence to a theistic framework, then the world Reality has no preordained "explanation," no underlying dogma at work. There is no theistic agenda. The Buddha himself made a point of telling one & all, "Do not take my word for this; experience it for yourself, & you will discover exactly what I have discovered." It was not "his" non-ego reality, it was *the* Reality of unconditioned awareness. We call it "Buddhist" because the Buddha's articulation is universally known & carefully detailed. If you experience the same Reality, it is "accidental" in the sense of "unexpected." ED had no special interest in Buddhism so far as is known, nor had she any inkling that ego-transcendence would transform her life forever. But the "accident" led to the inevitable, given her genius for articulating the stupendous drama of her inner life. As Awakened Mind she was the Buddha of Amherst.

ED's transcendent experience occurred within the confines of an American Protestant culture, but for her it transcended not only ego, but the collective ego of her society. I believe that her disinterest in any theological foundation was induced primarily by her sense of Oneness with Mother Nature. By this I mean Mother Nature in the form of her own Psyche – Mother Nature in the form of Emily Dickinson. This Oneness is full & complete, like a cornucopia, & has no room for Christianity as a patriarchal system of virtue & sin, of reward & punishment.

Ego-transcendence is the experience of ***ego–death***. This is a self-validating event. It becomes instantly evident that ego is an illusion created over time, created by accretion, as ED points out in P-970:

> Color-Caste-Denomination-
> These-are Time's Affair –

"Bliss" is one of ED's several terms for ego-transcendence.[1] When you savor the bliss of being centered in your own being, inevitably it will occur to you that suffering has vanished. Even if you are lying on a bed of pain, it will cease to "matter," so to speak. "You" no longer identify with the pain; the pain is there, but it is not "your" pain. Ego-transcendence liberates one from ego-suffering.

Thus the Four Noble Truths of the Buddha emerge naturally & effortlessly. The Buddha arranged them in this logical order:

1. Life is suffering
2. Suffering is caused by ego-attachments
3. Liberation from ego extinguishes ego-attachments
4. It is possible to live your life in such a way as to obtain liberation

Ego-transcendence as a sudden, unexpected event is the experience of the Third Noble Truth. This makes it clear that whatever is unsatisfactory about how you are arranging your life has to do with ego's leadership; for it is intent upon having its own way (First, Second Noble Truths). Then it dawns upon you that you don't have to keep kowtowing to ego; you can conduct

---

1 See poems 271, 338, 340, 343, 359, 1179, 1611.

your life differently in order to keep alive the spiritual vitality that has suddenly blossomed (Fourth Noble Truth).

It is obvious that no one can do this for you. You are in charge of your spiritual health. As the Zen adage puts it, "If you don't get it from yourself, where will you go for it?" So you will likely not "join a church," but rather embark upon a ***mindful*** life, ever aware of the ego-identity as an existential convenience, but not the ground of the world reality.

ED remained unaffiliated with any church, of course, but she continued to use Christian terminology. She called unconditioned awareness "God," & "Lord," but this should not lull us into thinking that she is a Christian poet, or even a fallen-away Christian poet.

ED also used "Master," & "Sire." Transcendentally they are synonyms for "God" & "Lord," whatever they may mean in a common, everyday sense. ED's commentators treat "Master" as a code word for a secret lover whom she didn't want to name. I call this the tabloid approach. The famous three "Master letters" excite a tabloid interest (were these letters actually sent to anyone?). What is important here, I think, is to distinguish between letters & poems. Emily Dickinson wrote the letters, but ED wrote the transcendentalist poems. Letters & poems are not a continuum, or common territory. Anyone can write a letter, but only ED can make an ED poem. Her "cryptic" style is not a code for her personal life, but rather the inevitable language of non-ego discourse.[2]

---

2 The 1952 anthology ***Poems of Emily Dickinson***, edited by Louis Untermeyer, represents the state of Dickinson studies in mid-twentieth century. In his introduction Untermeyer reviews the theories concerning ED's "love story," & the possible identity of her "mystery man," the frustrated love underlying the anguish of an "unrealized ecstasy" (xix). As if ED's transcendentalist poems were not brimming with ***realized*** ecstasy!

990

Not all die early, dying young -
Maturity of Fate
Is consummated equally
In Ages, or a Night -

A Hoary Boy, I've known to drop
Whole statured – by the side
Of Junior of Fourscore – 'twas Act
Not Period – that died.

AWAKENING TO LIFE: THE MATURITY OF FATE

It has long been apparent to me that ED's enlightenment was proactive, not reactive; it was not causally related to her time & place. She had not prepared for it, it just happened. There were no buddhas, no gurus available; the wisdom of awakening burst forth by itself. In P-990, "Not all die early," ED considers this phenomenon in the light of her own experience:

> Not all die early, dying young -
> Maturity of Fate
> Is consummated equally
> In Ages, or a Night -

"Maturity of Fate" is her name for her own sudden awakening, "consummated in a night" – "overnight," one might say. One day she was ignorant, & the next day was enlightened. One day she was a separate self in a given time & place, & the next day she was in the dharma. At first she didn't know what to make of it (might she be crazy?), but she soon recognized the truth of nonduality, & accepted that Maturity of Fate was a great gift bestowed upon her, as she says in an early poem (P-454):

> It was given to me by the Gods –
> When I was a little Girl –
> They give us Presents most – you know –
> When we are new – and small.

In the present poem she recognizes that one's chronological age at the time of death is irrelevant to one's spiritual progress on the path of life. I have know men in their twenties whom I considered to be "young fuddy-duddies" – "Hoary Boys," ED calls them.

If you do not seriously identify with the ego-identity assigned you, then you retain access to the archetypal Self, which is beyond clock time. It is neither young nor old; it is simply vital. At the chronological age of 80 one may simply be a "Junior of Fourscore."

So ED distinguishes between two kinds of death: Death of Act, & Death of Period. Obituary notices of elderly people may say, "died of natural causes," meaning that after a long period of time one just ups & dies. This is dying of old age – what ED calls here a "Period that dies."

On the other hand, vital people die in the act of living. This is the "Act that dies." For most people, to live means to stay in the rut of an ego-identity until their period of time is up. For people whose vitality cannot be contained by an ego-identity, living becomes spiritual action, or individuating. The sense of self is always evolving, day by day. Like Zen adepts, they seek to live in the Now.

So when a vital person dies, his or her effective action comes to an end. As ED puts it, 'twas Act that died. Living in the dharma, she already knew that clock time does not exist except for ego. When she became enlightened she knew that "Period" had died. Clock time ceased to exist, as she says in P-287, "A Clock stopped." Now she knows that whenever she dies she will simply be caught in the act of living. Enlightenment caught her in the act of non-living; death will catch her in the act of living.

THE SECRET LIFE

Ego-transcendence means the awakening of a new awareness, unfamiliar (or even alien) to the person's experience. It may come as a shock, & it may generate anxiety: is it friend or foe, benign or ominous?

Conrad Aiken's short story, "Silent Snow, Secret Snow," contains a lucid & eloquent description of the early stages of such an ambiguous consciousness as it unfolds in the mind of a twelve-year-old boy, Paul Hasleman. His first problem relates to his parents: the new experience "increasingly had brought him into a kind of mute misunderstanding, or even conflict, with his father and mother. It was as if he were trying to lead a double life." This could well be a description of ED's early experience of ego-transcendence, when she had to face the fact that she was living among egocentric people, ***including Emily Dickinson,*** all of whom would suspect some kind of pathology. In an early poem (410), she asks, "Could it be Madness – this?" This is a rhetorical question, to be sure, but in P-435 she recognizes that in the matter of "sanity,"

> "Tis the Majority
> In this, as All, prevail –
> Assent – and you are sane –
> Demur – you're straightway dangerous –
> And handled with a Chain –

In a late poem [1717] she continues to recognize the ego-identity as "that revolving reason / Whose esoteric belt / Protects our sanity." Aiken's protagonist immediately recognizes his dilemma:

> On the one hand he had to be Paul Hasleman, and keep up the appearance of being that person...; on the other, he had to explore this new world which had been opened to him. Nor could there be the slightest doubt...that the new world was the profounder and more wonderful of the two. It was irresistible. It was miraculous. Its beauty was simply beyond anything... But how then, between the two worlds, of which he was thus constantly aware, was he to keep a balance?

The boy is assaulted by the everyday, existential questions: "How was one to manage? How was one to explain? Would it be safe to explain? Would it be absurd? Would it merely mean that he would get into some obscure kind of trouble?"

ED herself surely reflected often on these same questions, always reaching the same, "tentative" conclusion: caution was her protection, the policy that kept her secret career alive & functioning. It unfolded in secrecy, as she created her poems & turned them into a hidden stash of handmade booklets, which she called her "slow riches" [P-843]. Their intrinsic value was evident, however obscurely, to her survivors, who intuited that these slow riches fully accounted for all the weirdness of the eccentric Lady in White.[3]

---

3 Aiken's "Silent Snow, Secret Snow," appears in the anthology ***Look Who's Talking*** [Bruce Weber, ed.], 155-173.

381

A Secret told –
Ceases to be a Secret – then –
A Secret – kept –
That - can appal but One –

Better of it – continual be afraid –
Than it –
And Whom you told it to – beside –

KEEPING IT SECRET

In a number of poems ED refers to ego-transcendence as both exhilarating & "appalling," as in P-281, "'Tis so appalling – it exhilarates," or in P-673, "'Tis this – invites – appalls," "convicts – enchants."

Emily Dickinson regarded ED as her secret identity, sometimes joyful, sometimes worrisome. Loss of ego-identity can be frightening when one is isolated in a community where such a thing appears tantamount to madness. Indeed, ED herself considered the matter more than once.[4] Even though she knew, in her heart of hearts, that she wasn't crazy, nevertheless her obvious "heresy," if made public, could be her undoing. A radical departure from the collective worldview could be regarded as subversive, as she has pointed out in P-435, quoted a few pages above:

> Assent – and you are sane –
> Demur – you're straightway dangerous –
> And handled with a Chain –

In the present poem Emily Dickinson ponders the advisability of letting the world in on her secret identity, the Secret Truth of her life. Loss of ego-identity in that provincial Victorian community was both "exhilarating" & "appalling," for it could strike fear into your heart, isolating you from the rest of humanity.

But there was no one with whom to share this burden, no guru, no possible confidant. If she were to reveal her Truth to

---

4 See poems 362, 410, 435, & 1717.

an egocentric person, then she would become vulnerable in ways not even imaginable:

> Better of it – continual be afraid –
> Than it –
> And Whom you told it to – beside

PARADOX, THE LANGUAGE OF TRANSCENDENTALISM

A paradox is a statement contrary to accepted opinion, seemingly contradictory or illogical. Transcendentalism abounds in paradox, and may even be its native source, like the speech of the ancient Greek oracles.

"Transcendentalism" refers to an actual experience, not to any doctrine or philosophy. This is the experience of ego-transcendence, when dual awareness becomes nondual awareness. Ego-speech depends on duality: "I/It," "I/you." Non-ego awareness cannot even be named (just call it the Tao, the Way). It cannot be "imagined" by an egocentric person, any more than erotic fulfillment can be "imagined" by a virgin. It is possible, however, to describe the dynamics of ego-transcendence in order to resolve the paradoxes expressed by the transcendentalists.

Since ego-transcendence is universal, this means that anyone who experiences it will use the same kind of language to talk about it, no matter from what culture, no matter from what century. This also means that the study of the poetry or sayings or sutras of any given transcendentalist is bound to involve ***comparative studies.*** The Buddha did not invent ego-transcendence, he simply awakened. That's all "buddha" means, after all – "awakened."

Throughout the twentieth century ED's poetry was much studied, and the Dickinsonian bibliography grows apace; yet no commentator I have read has yet recognized that ED was a buddha, that she awakened in Amherst; her critics appear to believe that she devoted her life to writing "cryptic," "puzzling" poems. What she was doing, however, was talking about transcendent matters that had been talked about innumerable times before her day – & there has been no letup since.

Ssu-hsin, a Chinese Zen master of the eleventh century, listed what he called the four "pivotal truths" of Ch'an (Zen):

1. There is life within death.
2. There is death within life.
3. There is permanent death in death.
4. There is permanent life in life[5]

These truths are explained logically as follows:

1. Unconditioned awareness (Life) arises when ego dies.
2. Ego-death can occur within one's lifetime. This is called Realization.
3. Physical death is permanent death of the person, both as body and as ego-self.
4. Realization can become a permanent part of one's life. This is called Actualization.

ED herself described the four pivotal truths in two terse poems, P-816, and P-1017:

A Death blow is a Life blow to Some
Who till they died, did not alive become –
Who had they lived, had died but when
They died, Vitality begun.

To die – without the Dying
And live – without the Life
This is the hardest Miracle
Propounded to Belief.

Can anyone distinguish between ED's words and those of Ssu-hsin?

---

5 *Teachings of Zen* (Thomas Cleary, tr.), 66.

1129

Tell all the Truth but tell it slant –
Success in Circuit lies
Too bright for our infirm Delight
The Truth's superb surprise

As Lightning to the Children eased
With explanation kind
The Truth must dazzle gradually
Or every man be blind –

Buddhism so kindness! So freedom! So special! Always say the truth. It's just natural. Everyone needs Buddha mind.

Tsung Tsai, Buddhist monk.
(*Tricycle*, Spring, 2000, 98)

POETRY OF THE DHARMA: THE TRUTH'S SUPERB SURPRISE

Tsung Tsai & ED (in the present poem) are both talking about nondual awareness. The monk simply praises it, but ED speaking to herself, recommends that she "tell it slant," for nondual awareness is alien to our cultural mainstream.

She recommends (& practices) circuitous discourse, consisting of paradox & metaphor. Her bliss & her liberation transcend that of egocentric happiness, which is "infirm." It is the same old frail thing, attachment to duality, "I/it," "I/you." ED describes her own awakening as "The Truth's superb surprise." Her task, as witness/poet, is to convey this Truth to an egocentric reader, by way of "kind explanations" in the form of striking language that can often be enjoyed even egocentrically.

Satori is lightning in the mind. It may "appal" (P-381), because the sudden death of the ego-self may raise the spectre of madness. ED suggests creating a "gradual dawning" (Buddhists recognize the existence of both sudden & gradual enlightenment). Perhaps long immersion in ED's poetry will make you eventually realize what she is talking about.

The last two lines seem to say that the Truth will blind, if suddenly sprung, whereas her poems will dazzle little by little. At the same time these two lines mean that if you don't gradually dazzle people with the Truth, then they will remain blind, or unawakened.

ED seems to have imagined an ideal reader, gradually led into nondual awareness by immersion in her poetry. In our profoundly dualistic society this is not likely to happen. Well over a century after her death, ED's poetry is still universally regarded as "cryptic" & "enigmatic." None of the considerable literature about ED's poetry (or about Emily Dickinson herself) even considers the possibility of ego-transcendence. This is bound to change, given the growing acceptance of American Buddhism into the mainstream.

1668

If I could tell how glad I was
I should not be so glad –
But when I cannot make the Force,
Nor mould it into Word,
I know it is a sign
That new Dilemma be
From mathematics further off
Than from Eternity.

69

Low at my problem bending,
Another problem comes –
Larger than mine – Serener –
Involving statelier sums.

I check my busy pencil,
My figures file away.
Wherefore, my baffled fingers
Thy perplexity?

Not when we know, the Power accosts –
The Garment of Surprise
Was all our timid Mother wore
At Home – in Paradise

(From P-1335)

LOGOS & EROS IN THE POETIC ENTERPRISE

In P-1668, "If I could tell," ED describes the dilemma facing the transcendentalist witness/poet: how to reconcile Logos & Eros, how to make them partners in the poetic enterprise. Eros is pure Life Force, sheer Becoming; Logos is naming, a static differentiating. The flowing river of time becomes a measurable phenomenon of seconds, minutes, & hours, of months & years, whereas ego-transcendence lifts you into the Eternal Now, where there is no "you." How can such an experience be captured in written words?

The first two lines of P-1668 show the poet playing with the subject pronoun:

> If I could tell how glad I was
> I should not be so glad –

For the transcendentalist there are always two referents for "I": the ego-dominant "I," & the ego-transcendent "I" – which is actually the eternally present Mind. In the first two lines of this poem the two referents may be expressed like this:

> If Emily Dickinson could tell how glad ED was
> Emily Dickinson/ED should not be so glad –

"Glad" is one of the many words used for ego-transcendence. Here, Emily Dickinson, speaking as poet/witness, muses on the dilemma which has always faced her: how to express Eros in terms of Logos. Her own private expression for this is "making the

Force." "Moulding it into Word," she adds. There have always been times when, as poet, she could not make the Force, & she takes this as a sign

> That new Dilemma be
> From mathematics further off
> Than from Eternity.

Ego-transcendence is "Eternity," & her poetic discourse wants to be farther & farther away from Logos (mathematics) & closer to Eternity. All her life she has worked with this challenge, which is what makes her poetry seem so "baffling" to egocentric readers. Each time she goes to make the Force she finds herself caught between the contrary demands of Eros & Logos. When she cannot make the Force she takes it as a sign that her expression "baffles" on the side of non-ego (Eternity) – i.e., it threatens to become unintelligible to egocentric people who rely on Logos.

P-69, a very early poem, expresses the difficulty described above. There she refers to the "mathematical" problem as one involving "statelier sums." Her "baffled fingers" are perplexed, reflecting the dilemma of the transcendentalist poet challenged to put down in writing (Logos) the experience of the Force (Eros).

The four lines from P-1335 illustrate ED's use of "Power" as a synonym for "Force"; when ego-transcendence occurs it is experienced as the Power, or Force, "accosting" the mind. This is always unexpected – it happens "Not when we know."

PUZZLED SCHOLARS

This World is not Conclusion,
A Species stands beyond...
It beckons, and it baffles...
To guess it, puzzles scholars...

(From P-501)

Professor Harold Bloom is the editor of the recent anthology, ***The Best Poems of the English Language*** (2004), and he includes a discussion of Emily Dickinson and her poetry.

Prof. Bloom is the most prestigious scholar I've read on this subject. He is currently Sterling Professor of Humanities at Yale; former Charles Eliot Norton Professor at Harvard; Shakespearean scholar, author of "more than 25 books," and recipient of numerous awards (this information comes from the jacket blurb). Therefore one must take note of what he has to say about Emily Dickinson and her poetry.

Prof. Bloom acknowledges that ED's poetry is baffling. Even though it "looks simple"' it is "very difficult," because she is so "cognitively original" (575). That is to say, ED's "cognition" is unique, seemingly impossible to get a handle on. Prof. Bloom says, "Though I read and teach her constantly, I remain a bewildered idolator, struggling to understand her enigmatic sublimities" (578).

In ***Solitary Prowess*** (20) we have quoted Prof. Cynthia Wolff's admission of puzzlement in her tome ***Emily Dickinson***: "...much of

Dickinson's strongest poetry is inaccessible – that is, it is difficult to determine precisely what such poetry is 'about'" (140). ED appears to be Prof. Wolff's wayward student:

> Had she couched her sentiments in lines that scanned and rhymed with regularity, the verse might be more accessible; had she been content with less radical compression of imagery or less violent ellipsis, her readers might tolerate the straining of traditional language more easily. Yet moderation did not figure in her plan. Perhaps she suffered from...self-limiting pride... (441)

The academic intellectual is set in his or her egocentric ways, accustomed to "mastering" the subject-matter in terms of a predetermined, rational vocabulary consistent with a dualistic grasp of reality. There is no alternative. If the subject-matter violates the dualistic premises, any presumed "context" vanishes. As Prof. Wolff puts it, one can no longer see what it is "about." Whenever "I study that" is replaced by "I *am* that," then ego is at sea.[6]

On the other hand (the one clapping?), nonego discourse speaks directly to nonego experience. For two millennia Eastern scholars of Buddhism have understood and commented on the sutras, simply because ***they know what they are talking about.*** An egocentric scholar discussing transcendentalist discourse literally does not know what he or she is talking about, and if honest, will admit to bafflement, like Profs. Wolff and Bloom. Bloom calls himself "a bewildered idolator, struggling to understand her enigmatic sublimities." This amuses ED: "Good to hide, and hear 'em hunt!" (P-842)

Prof. Bloom calls ED's poetry "the Gospel of Emily Dickinson"

---

6 *I Am That* (1973) is the title of the modern transcendentalist classic by Nisargadatta Maharaj.

– "Gospel," in the sense of "good news" (Gk. *euangélion*), as evangelists like to point out. But then he goes on to say that ED "has, though, no good news to proclaim. Despair, mourning and melancholia, psychic pain, erotic suffering: these are her *materia poetica*" (576). Is he talking about ED, or Edgar Allan Poe?

ED's primary subject is not suffering, but ego-transcendence, which is liberation from the stifling prison of the ego-self. This is her *materia poetica.*

PUZZLED READERS

> "Whatever is unintelligible would be certainly transcendental."
>
> -Charles Dickens in Boston, on his 1842 tour of America.[7]

ED's many fans are mostly ordinary readers who don't pretend to understand her puzzling language; in fact, they make a virtue out of it, which is easy to do. It is cryptic, compelling, & elegant, all at the same time. It is often Shakespearean, as in P-1384, "Praise it – 'tis dead":

> Invest this alabaster Zest
> In the Delights of Dust –
> Remitted – since it flitted it
> In recusance august.

This is bardic stuff – spellbinding, deeply satisfying – ***no matter what it may mean.*** "It is beauty that doesn't always ask for pure analysis."

That is how Brenda Hillman puts it, in her introduction to the small volume – a vade mecum – ***Emily Dickinson: Poems,*** one of the Shambhala Pocket Classics series. Hillman is a humanities teacher, not a scholar, & ED seems to be her favorite poet to

7 *American Notes for General Circulation* [see *Antiques Magazine* [Sept., 2003], 122.]

"teach." When her students confess puzzlement at the "strange diction," Hillman recommends a way to deal with it:

> Occasionally when students tell me it's hard to know how to read the poems, I tell them, read them quickly and let them shock you. If a line stays, read it again until you feel it is yours, and let the strange capital letters and the dashes carry the poems to the place in your unconscious that won't worry what they mean.[8]

I myself, as a humanities teacher with a different temperament, approached poems differently, for I would always "worry what they mean." Well, maybe not "worry"; I would "wonder what they mean," wonder where the poet was coming from, that he or she could say these things all new to me. It made me feel that my understanding of life was very limited, & that the poet, as an oracle, could raise my consciousness. The poem was a koan, & it was my task to focus on a reality more sophisticated than what I was used to calling "real." I felt that the oracle was opening the "doors of perception," & that it was up to me to somehow imagine my way through those doors.

But that's just how I am, & why I am writing these pages. Others enjoy the very mystery of oracular poets, & this I can understand – for to be enjoyably puzzled by ED is to be enjoyably puzzled by life itself.

---

8 Hillman, xiv.

645

Bereavement in their death to feel
Whom We have never seen –
A Vital Kinsmanship import
Our Soul and theirs – between –

For Stranger – Strangers do not mourn –
There be Immortal friends
Whom Death see first – 'tis news of this
That paralyze Ourselves –

Who, vital only to Our Thought –
Such Presence bear away
In dying – 'tis as if Our Souls
Absconded – suddenly –

INDRA'S NET, THE ROOT OF COMPASSION

ED, the "not-self," intuited the ecological Oneness of the phenomenal world. "Ecology" is a commonly understood idea today, though even fifty years ago, very few people had ever heard of an ecosystem. Today a sophisticated idea like the "butterfly effect" has even made its way into the dictionaries.

The idea that all the organisms in an environment are vitally interconnected seems to rise naturally into ego-transcendent awareness. Ego-mind is dual, creating a separateness between itself & the world "out there." Indeed, this is the only way ego-mind can exist. Ego-transcendence obliterates this duality, & each transcendentalist makes this discovery anew. Anyone can grasp the *idea* of ecology, but actually to experience oneself as part of an ecosystem requires an awakening from the anti-ecological isolation of ego. For ego, our skin is an armor; for non-ego it is a porous sponge.

When ED made this discovery she used the notion of "kinsmanship" to talk about it, as she does in the present poem: "A Vital Kinsmanship." As a Zen gardener she had always been aware of the Unity of Nature, of the bee & the rose as related, like kinsmen. In P-1709 she says that each year Autumn is "Invited to return" by "influential kinsmen." In P-885 she calls the worms "Our little Kinsmen." In P-380 she calls the grass "Near Kinsman to" a flower. In P-1137 she says, "The kinsmen of the Wind are Peaks..."

The younger ED was a warmly social person, & it was not difficult for her (as for St. Francis) to think of the critters & plants in her world as her extended family, her kinsmen.

This whole idea has been part of the Hindu experience since ancient times, in the form of Indra's Net, eventually adopted by Buddhist teachers as expressive of the "universal biome." Indra, the supreme Hindu god, is said to have a Net – a Net that we call the world, or the universe. At each intersection of the Net is a jewel, a specific being, whether person, plant, critter, or even phenomenon, that reflects all the other jewels in the Net. All of us mirror each other, & no one is anything else than this reflection. Ego-mind does not want to look into this mirror; in fact, its existence depends upon ***not*** looking into it. In order to exist ego needs samsara, the world of separate individuals unconnected:

> Despite our apparent existence in separate "skin bags" (as Zen expresses it), we are actually one with everything in the universe. The notion that we are individual selves is simply a convenient illusion, one that helps us survive in the world of samsara.
> On a deeper level, the image of Indra's Net suggests that we have a responsibility to think and act for the benefit of everything in the universe. The care we give to this endeavor is simultaneously for our own good as well as the good of others.[9]

In the present poem ED says that when you feel compassionately connected with the world, you experience a "vital" kinsmanship. "Vital" means "visceral," an "import" [significance] between "Our Soul and theirs" [lines 3-4]. Those strangers are not really strangers, because to the compassionate heart no thing is a stranger.

In this poem ED uses "vital" twice, in line 3 ("Vital Kinsmanship") & in line 9, "vital only to Our Thought." The death of a bird,

---

9 Jack Maguire, ***Essential Buddhism***, 135.

a worm, a tree, a flower – this is a death "vital *only* to Our Thought," not to our actual family in the world of samsara. This Thought is compassionate awareness.

1053

It was a quiet way –
He asked if I was his –
I made no answer of the Tongue
But answer of the Eyes –
And then He bore me on
Before this mortal noise
With swiftness, as of Chariots
And distance, as of Wheels.
This World did drop away
As Acres from the feet
Of one that leaneth from Balloon
Upon an Ether street.
The Gulf behind was not,
The Continents were new –
Eternity it was before
Eternity was due.
No Seasons were to us –
It was not Night nor Morn –
But Sunrise stopped upon the place
And fastened it in Dawn.

TRANSCENDENTALIST LOVE POETRY

Transcendentalist poetry often reads like profane love poetry, as we know from the Song of Solomon, the lyrics of Rumi, or of San Juan de la Cruz. Whether such poetry is sacred or profane is often inferred from our knowledge of the life of the poet. If little is known of the poet's inner, spiritual life, then such poetry may be understood literally as "erotic."

Such is the case with ED. None of the commentators I have read know or suspect her of being an authentic mystic in the non-sectarian tradition of transcendentalism. ED's commentators appear to be innocent of knowledge or interest in the subject of Enlightenment, evidently because they do not think it relevant to the writings of Emily Dickinson. Thus ED's famous "erotic" poem "Wild Nights" (P-249) impresses readers as a literal reference to a roll in the hay. This is a gratuitous impression.

The present poem, "It was a quiet way," may be useful in dispelling the idea that ED's "love poetry" refers to secret sexual activity, because here she uses traditional expressions of spiritual intimacy that evoke sexual intimacy. Physical orgasm & spiritual orgasm are analogous, so the latter must not be thought of as a "metaphor" for the former; the same language describes them both.

The first two lines of this poem could come from any popular love ballad. They may seem "profane" because of ED's reference to a man: "He asked if I was his." But "he" & "him" (like "man" & "mankind") are not necessarily gender specific in ED's writing (or in that of any other nineteenth-century writer).

ED makes a point of contrasting "quiet" (line 1) with "noise" (line 6). This is a major issue in ego-transcendence (as in formal meditation), because the constant noise of the ego-world militates against inner peace, as ED says in P-1251:

> Silence is all we dread.
> There's Ransom in a Voice –
> But Silence is Infinity.
> Himself have not a face.

The present poem describes merging with Buddha Mind. When ego falls away, Buddha Mind appears to beckon hospitably, like a genial host, as in P-1721:

> He was my host – he was my guest,
> I never to this day
> If I invited him could tell,
> Or he invited me.
>
> So infinite our intercourse
> So intimate, indeed,
> Analysis as capsule seemed
> To keeper of the seed.

(By "capsule" I understand "spore sac"; ego-intellect contains the seed, but is not part of it.)

Ego-transcendence is well named, because to transcend is to fly upward, or to be borne aloft, as in a balloon in this poem or in P-700, "You've seen Balloons set – Haven't You?" One is carried aloft, beyond the "mortal noise" (line 6) of the everyday world.

The matter of noise vs. silence is basic to the transcendentalist experience, & recalls Timothy Leary's famous admonition to "turn on, tune in, & drop out." When one transcends ("turns on," chemically or naturally), one tunes in to the non-ego wave length & drops away from the "mortal noise." This din is both the noise of the everyday world, & the noise of the chattering ego. What ED says in this poem, beginning in line 9, "This World did drop away," describes the classic experience of ego-transcendence in terms of getting beyond the "mortal noise" of the everyday life that besets us all. Here it is worth quoting a similar description by a contemporary transcendentalist, Fleet Maull.

Fleet Maull is a longtime Buddhist adept & activist who did fourteen years time in prison. Like ED, he realized that he had to escape the mortal noise of his prison (see ED's poem 652, "A Prison gets to be a friend"): he could either identify with his prison, or he could transcend it:

> I started practicing meditation...almost immediately. One evening, many months into my sentence, I realized that my mind was not moving. I was calm and my mind was steady. Regardless of the noise and anger around me, my mind was not pulled by it. I had had these kinds of experiences before, but in a quiet Buddhist retreat center. To find it in the midst of those circumstances was liberating.[10]

As ED puts it in the present poem, "This World did drop away." She finds herself "Upon an Ether street," in the Eternal Now, as in P-287, "A Clock stopped." Sunrise (line 19), as a moment in clock time, becomes Dawn (last line), meaning Enlightenment.[11]

---

10 Fleet Maull, "Practice with the Cell," ***Parabola***, (Summer, 2003), 26. Maull is the founder of Prison Dharma Network.

11 Why the "Ether" metaphor? Ether distances one from (ego-)suffering – indeed, from all ego-involvements. See Thoreau's description of the ether experience (***Journal***, May 12, 1851), quoted in ***Solitary Prowess***, 231.

1071

Perception of an object costs
Precise the Object's loss –
Perception in itself a Gain
Replying to its Price –
The Object Absolute – is nought –
Perception sets it fair
And then upbraids a Perfectness
That situates so far –

PERCEPTION IN ITSELF

This poem is an analysis of Perception, which of course involves both ego-perception & ego-transcendent perception. To perceive an object transcendentally means to experience its "suchness," as in most classical haiku. When this occurs, the object is "lost" (line 2) as a substantial thing "out there," in relation to ego. It merges with the mind, as in Basho's famous haiku:

> The old pond;
> a frog jumps in –
> splash!

One might say that the frog leaps with a sudden splash into the mind experienced as an ancient, deep pond of water.[12]

Ego sees every object – & every person – in relation to itself, naturally. This relativity is "precisely" what is lost when an object shines forth in its surreal suchness. "Perception in itself" (line 3) is ED's term for this phenomenon, which the Buddhists call ***tathata,*** a key concept in the Buddhist teaching of human psychology (the ***abhidharma***). Ego-loss is the "Price" you pay for the Gain of Buddha Mind.

The suchness of an object is what ED calls "The Object Absolute" (line 5) – no longer relative. Experienced as such it is "nought," which is to say that it has no independent existence (just as the ego-self has none). One now experiences Truth as Beauty, the "perfectness" of the transcendent reality. When you come

12 ED herself speaks of the mind as a well, as in P-460 ("a little Well – like Mine"); see especially her richly detailed P-1400 & P-1712.

back down from the experience you may "upbraid," or regret the great distance it seems from everyday ego-perception. It is a "Sudden Guest" [P-1309] that seems to come & go fitfully.

Pure Perception reveals what the Buddhists call *anicca,* the not-self of phenomenal reality. This becomes the subject of a number of poems by ED, a few of which are discussed in the following section.

IMPERMANENCE (ANICCA)

> Burning destroys nothing. It just shuffles the molecules.
>
> (Old chemical slogan)

The core meanings of Buddhist discourse are determined by ego-transcendent experiences of Reality. When this discourse is translated into English, it is inevitably read from an egocentric viewpoint (the same is true of ED's poetic discourse). ***Anicca,*** "impermanence," – a basic term in the Buddhist discourse – offers a prime example of this cross-cultural confusion.

When the Buddhist states that everything is "impermanent," the Westerner sees no reason to disagree, because this seems obvious to any observer, East or West. One need only watch things live & die, or study the fossil records of life on earth: nothing lasts forever.

But the meaning of anicca is not confined to any such obvious fact of life. Anicca refers to the impermanence, or non-existence of any "thing in itself." The rainbow is a good example: the Westerner has no difficulty grasping that the rainbow is not a thing, in the sense that the oak tree is a thing; it is an optical illusion, "impermanent," not because it is ephemeral, but because it doesn't exist apart from the refraction & reflection of the sun's rays in raindrops. It is a mirage.

In the West, "permanent" means "enduring in stable form," as an oak tree or a housefly does. We all understand that while the oak or the fly achieves a stable – mature – form, it too, is finally impermanent, meaning that it has a limited lifespan.

But ego-transcendence reveals a reality beyond the question of longevity. The oak is "impermanent" in the same sense that the rainbow is impermanent. As a "thing," it is made up of atoms; & just as the atom is not a thing – a tiny, indivisible particle – so any thing made up of atoms is likewise "no-thing." This is the Void of which the Buddhists speak, as this is expressed in the Heart Sutra (chanted daily throughout the Buddhist world):

> Form is no other than emptiness, emptiness is no other than form. Form is exactly emptiness, emptiness exactly form. Sensation, conception, discrimination, awareness are likewise like this. ...all dharmas are forms of emptiness: not born, not destroyed, not stained, not pure, without loss, without gain.[13]

When you see an oak tree, think of it as a "rainbow oak," an illusion like that of the rainbow, only lasting longer in clock time. Like the atom itself, it has no substantial, solid self.

Theoretically the liberal-minded Westerner might be able to grant the fundamental truth of anicca, even if not experiencing it personally; but when anicca it applied to the ego-self, then a big problem arises. This is because the ego-self, as an enduring, permanent "thing," is ***self-evident,*** evident to itself: ego thinks, therefore ego is (***ego cogito ergo ego sum***). It has no way of deconstructing the wall of separation between itself & the world "out there." All Westerners recognize that each human life on earth is impermanent, but when the person eventually dies, the ego-self is believed to survive as a soul, & to go to an afterlife, where it will abide "permanently."

Westerners believe in the survival of a "permanent" soul, even when death is premature. Children are changing day by day as they grow into adults; but if the child should suddenly die, then the Westerner believes that the ego-self as soul instantly becomes "permanent," & goes to heaven, where it will await the eventual arrival of its grief-stricken parents. All of this is taken

13 Quoted in Maguire, 79.

"on faith," of course. Many Western pet owners even believe that their deceased dogs & cats have permanent ego-selves awaiting them in heaven.

With ego-transcendence anicca is experienced as a reality, part of an awareness unconditioned by the local boundaries of the ego-self. The conditioned ego-self is seen to be a pseudo-reality, like a rainbow, conditioned by the reflections & refractions of a local culture.

In our commentary "Amazing Grace" (see above, p.17), we have noted how Buddha Mind enabled ED to write of "impermanence" as she does in P-1257 ("Dominion lasts until obtained"): of the morning dew, that most transient of phenomena, she says,

> How everlasting are the Lips
> Known only to the Dew –
> These are the Brides of permanence
> Supplanting me and you.

All recurring natural phenomena are "permanently" part of Nature's eternal Becoming, whereas the individual ego-self occurs only once, never again (certainly not in any "afterlife"). The ego-self stands apart from Nature, & relates to Her as the Other – something to be dominated or possessed (or avoided). Dominion & possession are typically a part of the ego-self, as stated in the first stanza of this poem:

> Dominion lasts until obtained –
> Possession just as long –
> But these – endowing as they flit
> Eternally belong.

Dominion & possession "Eternally belong" to ego's basic

experience of itself; they "endow" ego with a sense of its own reality – but this is a fleeting (or "flitting") illusion.

985

The Missing All – prevented Me
From missing minor Things.
If nothing larger than a World's
Departure from a Hinge –
Or Sun's extinction, be observed –
'Twas not so large that I
Could lift my Forehead from my work
For Curiosity.

All that we are arises with our thoughts.
With our thoughts we make the world.

—the Buddha

NIRVANA ("EXTINCTION")

"To miss" has a number of meanings, two of which apply in the present poem: (1) to fail to perceive (be unconscious of), & (2) to regret the absence or loss of.

The Buddhist readily understands that the ego-self is "missing the All," meaning the Oneness of world & mind. In order even to exist, ego demands a dual reality, I/world, inner world/outer world. Thus understood, the first two lines of the present poem say, "The ego-self, unaware of the higher Self (the All), prevented me from missing the absence of everything 'out there' in the world." A second possible meaning: "It prevented me from overlooking the absence of everything out there." "Everything" – each "thing" – exists only as a concept, one of the "thoughts" with which we make the world.

"If nothing larger" (line 3) means "anything less." "Anything less than a cosmic event could not even excite my curiosity." This is true of us all: we do not question the ontological premises of the ego-self. Everything in the "outer" reality is regarded as a permanent entity, just as we believe the ego-self to be substantial.

> Rather than *see* the wind, or waves – or a stream or a cup or a book – as the constant flux that each is, we imagine them to be solid, persisting, separate...things. We attribute

> this "thingness" to them in the same way that we attribute selfhood to human beings.[14]

This passage, from Hagen's book on Buddhism, concludes with the observation that applies to the present poem:

> Instead of ***seeing*** the thoroughgoing motion, flux, and flow of experience, we imagine a vast proliferation of innumerable, separated things. In short, we grant selfhood to whatever we find "out there."

The selfhood of the things we find "out there" is what ED means by the "minor Things" of our egocentric reality.

Ego-transcendence reveals the Big Picture, the All, which is Oneness. Egocentric reality consists of an endless number of "minor things." You can't "miss" them, they are obvious, nor can you miss their absence. This is because the ego-self regards them as solidly present. Ego-transcendence, however, makes the ego-self vanish – poof! With this, all the "substantial" things & ideas of the "substantial" self also vanish.

The "cosmic event" (lines 3-5) is ego-transcendence, the "transvaluation of values," that unhinges the egocentric world & extinguishes the Apollonian view of the world reality. Ego-transcendence is nirvana, which simply means "extinction" of the ego-self. When it occurs one may suddenly ***see*** how there is no "thing" out there. Every "thing" is a shimmering presence, like a rainbow, a Becoming. It seems a miracle that these shapes can steadily cohere. Such is the flux, the absence of all selfhood that the Buddhist & Hindu adepts have been experiencing down through the centuries. This is the "World's Departure" from the sense of reality that hinges on our illusion of innumerable, separated things.

---

14 Steve Hagen, ***Buddhism Plain and Simple,*** 134-5.

ED's ego-transcendent experiences gave birth to her poetic style, as in this poem, notable for its lack of "form," avoidance of punctuation, & the freedom she took with established usage. I think of it as the Liberated, or Nirvanic Style.

1499

How firm Eternity must look
To crumbling men like me
The only Adamant Estate
In all Identity –

How mighty to the insecure
Thy Physiognomy
To whom not any Face cohere –
Unless concealed in thee

What is your original face, the one you had before your parents were born?

Famous Zen koan

YOUR ORIGINAL FACE (1)

In this poem ED refers to herself in the masculine, which is not unusual for her,[15] or for the times, when "men," "man," & "mankind" commonly meant "everybody." When she says "men like me" (line 2) she means "people like me"; certainly she did not have in mind "women like me."

This is a poem about the identity crisis commonly provoked by the experience of ego-transcendence: "Who am I?" One's received ego-identity is "insecure" per se, & it "crumbles" in the face of the higher Self. The illusory ego is experienced as the "Nobody" of P-288 ("I'm Nobody! Who are you?")[16] In the present poem ED states that Eternity appears as a "firm" Identity, an "Adamant Estate," or condition of life – unchanging, hard as steel or diamond (L. *adamantinus*).

The transcendentalist experiences the ego-identity as insubstantial & illusory, by contrast to the "Physiognomy" of the higher Self, which is the Faceless Face, the Face of Faces to which "not any (ego-) Face cohere." One's transcendent identity turns out to have been concealed all the time in the Face of the Higher Self, i.e. the Presence of the Higher Self. As such, this poem is an appropriate response to the Zen koan quoted above.

---

15 See, for example, P-1466, "...I am a rural man," P-389, "...I used to – when a Boy," or P-466, "I...who am the Prince of Mines."

16 See our discussion of P-288 in *Solitary Prowess*, 98-100.

1090

I am afraid to own a Body –
I am afraid to own a Soul –
Profound – precarious Property –
Possession, not optional –

Double Estate – entailed at pleasure
Upon an unsuspecting Heir –
Duke in a moment of Deathlessness
And God, for a Frontier.

YOUR ORIGINAL FACE (2)

From childhood on we learn to live life as a dual reality, beginning with the "ego/world," or "I/it" reality. "I" live ***in*** the "world," & this duality seems to be self-evident.

We also learn to live life as a mind/body or soul/body duality – so much so that we accept the orthodox religious worldview that when we die, only the body dies, whereas the soul survives in heaven or hell as an ego-identity, just as depicted in Dante's ***Divine Comedy,*** or in the Baptist hymn, "When the roll is called up yonder I'll be there!"

That notion is based on a conflation of "ego-identity" & "soul," an idea satirized in P-215, "What is – "Paradise" - / Who live there." Using the voice of a naïve little girl ED asks if there are farmers in heaven, & do they hoe? (If so then Mother Earth Herself must go to heaven so that they may hoe Her.)

Anyone who has experienced ego-transcendence learns right away that the ego-identity is a useful & practical mode of consciousness that enables us to deal with everyday life in our community, but it is not substantially real. Beginning with Gautama Buddha, every Buddhist adept has passed on the message: "Don't take my word for it, do it yourself! To awaken from the illusion of the ego-self is the rightful destiny of every human being."

In the present poem ED addresses this issue of the dual reality accepted as "real" by her entire community. Her own experience tells her differently, & in the first stanza she critiques it:

I am afraid to own a Body –
I am afraid to own a Soul –
Profound – precarious Property –
Possession, not optional –

She is loath to continue embracing the dual reality, because if you do this, then the "you," the ego-self, has no choice but to believe that "you" own your body & soul, i.e., that body & soul have an "owner," a "possessor." This is a necessary part of the illusion; it is not "optional." The conventional citizen says, "I have a body, & I have a soul." This seems self-evident. But ED as a transcendentalist, knows that ego's idea of "self-evident" is folly, because ego is in no way evident to the Self.

Stanza two points out that this "Double Estate" (the "ablative" – practical – estate of P-1741) is passed on from generation to generation, like a family heirloom willed to the children: "I'm proud that my kids are real New Englanders!" This double estate is "entailed at pleasure / Upon an unsuspecting Heir."

Upon an unsuspecting Heir. This is one of ED's most trenchant lines, evoking the koan, "What is your original face, the one you had before your parents were born?" It is your original non-ego awareness, before your parents passed on to you your cultural social identity (i.e., *their* cultural social identity).

Ego-transcendence raises you beyond the learned ego-identity, it "ennobles" you "in a moment of Deathlessness." You become a "Duke" – or "Prince" (P-959), or "Majesty" (P-290), or "Monarch" (P-642), or "King" (P-803), or "Queen" (P-285), or "Autocrat" (P-306), or "Emperor" (P-980), etc. You become ennobled, with "God, for a Frontier" – limitless.

1315

Which is the best – the Moon or the Crescent?
Neither – said the Moon –
That is best which is not – Achieve it –
You efface the Sheen.

Not of detention is Fruition –
Shudder to attain.
Transport's decomposition follows –
He is Prism born.

1255

Longing is like the Seed
That wrestles in the Ground,
Believing if it intercede
It shall at length be found.

The Hour, and the Clime –
Each Circumstance unknown,
What Constancy must be achieved
Before it see the Sun!

BEING & BECOMING: SELF & NOT-SELF

The not-self (anicca) of all things, including ego, is the world of ***Becoming.*** It transcends the illusory world of ***Being,*** to which the ego is firmly addicted. Liberation from this addiction allows creative activity to enter into one's everyday life. It made possible ED's poetic achievement throughout some thirty-five years free of the ego-tyranny that keeps most of us in a rut.

For ED, the greatest joy in life was the creative act itself, not its result – what the Buddhists call Samadhi Play. Samadhi ("trance") is one-pointed, focused attention on the process of transcendent Becoming, a birth of consciousness. In the present poem, P-1315, ED contrasts ego-enjoyment of one's poetry (the "Fruition of detention") to non-ego enjoyment of the creative act itself. By Samadhi Play one "attains" a result, but the real issue is the ecstatic trip itself, which is its own orgasmic reward, a Happening, fireworks going off in a mind engaged with the heart.

In this poem ED treats the Moon as an oracle, and asks her question: "Which is the best – the Moon or the Crescent?" This is actually a leading question which means, "which is best: Being or Becoming?" ("Crescent" is from L. ***crescens,*** "growing".) The answer is "Neither." The lunar oracle says, "That is best, which is not." ED explains this in an earlier poem, P-1255 (quoted here along with P-1315), where she says that her life is driven by a "longing," an unknown seed in the ground. It is both Being & Becoming "which is not," because it abides in the Creative Unconscious, intuited but unknown. One's life becomes a drive to "Achieve it":

What Constancy must be achieved
Before it see the Sun!

"Achievement," is samadhi play itself, not the product of samadhi play. The "Sheen" of the moon, its shining, is what Wallace Stevens calls "the intelligence of our sleep."[17] Her open eye allows us to go beyond, to do something, rather than to passively admire.

When an inspiration has been expressed in the form of a poem, then it is held in check forever – in "detention" (Line 5) – as are all the poems in the ED canon. Fortunately for us, all her poems are "in custody" – but that has nothing to do with her being engrossed in creating them. For ED "publication" was neither here nor there, for that is a dreary activity of ego-ambition, as she says in P-709:

Publication – is the Auction
Of the Mind of Man –
Poverty – be justifying
For so foul a thing

"Shudder to attain," she says (present poem, line 6), contrasting attainment with the Fruition (enjoyment) of Becoming, not the fruition of admiring a completed poem. To enjoy attainment, i.e., to rest on one's laurels, is a waste of energy. It is an ego-activity that paralyzes "Transport" (line 7). Transport, creative exhilaration, gives life its human dimension; gathering the quiet white light of the moon, it is "Prism born." Transport shatters light into all the colors of the rainbow. It "effaces the Sheen" (see line 4).

ED makes a point of crediting the Moon Herself with this

17 In "Someone puts a Pineapple Together." See ***The Necessary Angel.***

epiphany. She consulted "the intelligence of her sleep," & this poem is the answer she got.[18]

18 What we say here about the self-sufficiency of samadhi play applies equally to Joseph Cornell (1903-72), the self-taught genius now recognized as one of the great innovators of 20th-century American art. Even after art dealers began to woo him in the 1960s, the very private Cornell remained uncooperative, deeply reluctant to share his art with the world at large. Anyone interested in the "introverted genius" of ED should study Cornell's work & read Deborah Solomon's absorbing biography of Cornell, ***Utopia Parkway.*** (One of Cornell's shadow boxes, "Towards the Blue Peninsula," from 1953, is dedicated to ED & her P-405, "It might be lonelier.")

1563

By homely gift and hindered Words
The human heart is told
Of Nothing –
"Nothing" is the force
That renovates the World –

> Thanks to impermanence, everything is possible. Life itself is possible. If a grain of corn is not impermanent, it can never be transformed into a stalk of corn. ... If your daughter is not impermanent, she cannot grow up to become a woman. ...welcome and long live impermanence.
>
> —Thich Nhat Hanh[19]

Anicca, "impermanence," is a fundamental tenet of Buddhist thought: all conditioned phenomena, "things that come into being dependent on causes and conditions," are transient.[20] This includes the ego-self, of course, which is no different from any other conditioned thing in this respect. Like the atom itself, every "thing" composed of atoms is energy. The atom is not a hard, indivisible particle (as used to be thought), nor is any "thing" that is made up of atoms. Conditioned reality is "no-thing."

Ego-transcendence makes this clear by revealing that the ego-self is nothing. The present poem is based on this empirical insight.

The poem actually begins as poetry criticism. ED was always aware that her poetry differed radically from the egocentric verse that passed for poetry in her day, the poetic equivalent of a Norman Rockwell reality. The talent to write such poetry is what

---

19 Quoted in ***Shambhala Sun*** (Nov 2002), 31. The venerable Thich Nhat Hanh, a Vietnamese Buddhist master, is a world leader in activist Buddhism; Martin Luther King, Jr., nominated him for the Nobel Peace Prize.

20 Damien Keown, ***A Dictionary of Buddhism,*** art. "anitya."

ED calls, in the present poem, a "homely gift." Popular "fireside poetry" was composed of "hindered words," clichéd speech that can tell the human heart nothing. Of the "nature poets" popular at the time she observed, in P-1400,

> But nature is a stranger yet;
> The ones that cite her most
> Have never passed her haunted house,
> Nor simplified her ghost.

(I take "simplify" to mean "reveal the essentials, make easier to understand".)

ED, in the present poem (with her usual sense of ambiguity), picks up on the word "nothing": popular poetry tells the heart "nothing" at all, for it plays with surface meanings. Like Norman Rockwell, it treats everyday life as a solid, enduring phenomenon.

But ego-transcendence reveals every cultural entity to be a "no thing," like the snows of yesteryear. It also reveals the ego-self to be nothing more than transient energy. It is this very anicca that allows ego-transcendence to occur, & this "is the force / That renovates the World." ED's use of "renovate" echoes the traditional mystics' term, ***renovatio***, the Renewal of Reality that takes place when the nothingness of ego stands revealed.

ED AS ACCIDENTAL BUDDHIST

803

Who Court obtain within Himself
Sees every Man a King –
And Poverty of Monarchy
Is an interior thing –

No Man depose
Whom Fate Ordain –
And Who can add a Crown
To Him who doth continual
Conspire against His Own

EVERYONE A KING, EVERYONE A BUDDHA: DO NOT CONSPIRE AGAINST YOUR OWN!

> In his final talk before his death the Buddha said, "Each of you be a light unto yourself; betake yourself to no external refuge. Hold fast to the Truth. Look not for refuge to anyone beside yourself."[21]

Unlike theistic religions Buddhism teaches that each person carries within the final spiritual authority, the ultimate guru, because each person is a potential buddha, potentially an "awakened one." When you awaken you must see that everybody can awaken. Gautama Buddha is not a "god," but simply a model in the quest for enlightenment. Anyone may experience the fact that the ego-identity has no ontological credibility.

In the present poem ED herself makes this point just as clearly as Gautama Buddha himself. After all, it is the most natural thought in the world, if one has awakened. The first stanza of this poem can be reworded as follows:

> Whoever enlightenment obtain within himself
> sees every man a buddha,
> for dearth of buddhahood
> is an interior thing.

This aphoristic poem is one of many by ED that I regard not simply as a "poem," but as a sutra. She is stating a fact obvious to

---

21 Steve Hagen, ***Buddhism Plain and Simple***, 21.

an awakened person, but vague – even esoteric – to egocentric people.

Here, as elsewhere, ED refers to buddha mind as "king," "monarch," "emperor," etc. In P-980 she says:

> Purple – is fashionable twice –
> This season of the year,
> And when a soul perceives itself
> To be an Emperor.

This theme is as essential to the oeuvre of ED as it is to Buddhism itself.

The second stanza states a basic principle of individuation: one's inner buddha, or enlightened Self, is what ED calls one's "Own" (last line). This is your birthright as a human being, your most precious potential. Naturally the ego-identity shuts itself off from ego-transcendence (its own demise). This is what ED calls in the last two lines, "continually conspiring." Anyone who practices meditation finds this out right away: ego-mind is continually conspiring against non-ego mind.

In this second stanza ED admonishes us:

> No Man depose
> Whom Fate Ordain –

"Depose" refers to king, of course. The "Man" we must not depose is the inner Self, the one who can "add a Crown" to the everyday ego-awareness (who is continually conspiring against "His Own").

ED fully recognizes that enlightenment is a Grace, a gift, like manna from heaven. If it happens to you, it means that Fate has "ordained" your higher (or deeper) Self. "Ordain" here means "make holy." Let us rephrase ED's admonishment:

Do not unthrone the Self
whom Fate ordain,
the One who can crown
him who continually
conspires against the Self, his Own.

713

Fame of Myself, to justify,
All other Plaudit be
Superfluous – An Incense
Beyond Necessity –

Fame of Myself to lack – Although
My Name be else Supreme –
This were an Honor honorless –
A futile Diadem –

FAME OF ONESELF: THE INDIVIDUATION PROCESS

The Individuation Process, identified & studied in detail by Jung, refers to the lifelong process whereby you, born as an evolved, higher animal, inherit the ability transmitted by Nature to continue evolving individually, on your own.[22]

You are born & reared in a given society, & you develop a local ego-identity in terms of that society, including language, gender, ideology, religion, & all the rest. In order to develop your own unique individuality, your deeper (or higher) Self, you must transcend the "mass-produced" ego-identity. The most extreme form of individuation is that practiced by the Buddhists, taking as their inspiration Gautama Buddha. Theistic religions identify the not-self with their particular god(s), but Buddhism sees this as one final form of conditioned awareness. It is arbitrary & unnecessary to assign a name & theology to the not-self; "Impossible to name it, I just call it the Tao, the Way," says Lao Tzu (*Tao Te Ching*, ch. 25).

ED assigned different names to the not-self – Lord, God, Master, Sire, even Jupiter (P-1730) – but also referred to it in the abstract, as Noon, Sun, Circle, or simply identified its affective nature – exhilaration, transport, ecstasy, bliss, etc.

Since ED & Emily Dickinson shared a dual life as "mutual Monarch" (P-642), there was a basic ongoing awareness of the Individuation Process (how could there not be?). In P-856 she calls this the Eternal Function; in the present poem she calls it "Fame of Myself."

The alternative to achieving Fame of Oneself ("Fame of Myself

---

22 This evokes the principle that "ontogeny recapitulates phylogeny."

to lack") would be to achieve ego-fame ("Although / My Name be else Supreme"); but this would be an honorless Honor (line 7), as ED points out elsewhere, especially in her poems on the spiritual futility of fame as defined by the "admiring Bog" (P-288)[23]

Intrapsychic "Fame," or glory, means redemption of the Higher Self, buried under all the debris of the ego-identity. It means connecting with the basic reality of Psyche. The revelation of this process throughout the oeuvre of ED is what stirs me to regard her as an Accidental Buddhist.[24]

---

23 See poems 866, 1232, 1379, 1475, 1659, & 1763.

24 "Fame of Oneself" is also the guiding principle of the ***Tao Te Ching,*** where the enlightened consciousness is a great non-ego ruler governing Psyche.

1370

Gathered into the Earth,
And out of story –
Gathered to that strange Fame –
That lonesome Glory
That hath no omen here – but Awe –

STRANGE FAME, LONESOME GLORY

In the present poem ED says of ego-transcendence, it "hath no omen here – but Awe." An omen is a sign intuited as prophetic, revealing a transcendent truth. This is a self-validating experience; as ED says, in P-356 ("The Day that I was crowned"), "I rose, and all was plain." This induces a powerful sense of awe, an exhilarating intuition of the Immediate Truth, & it is this very awe that validates the experience: it "hath no omen here – but Awe."

For ED it was a "lonesome Glory," of course, because she couldn't share it with anyone else. In a conservative Christian community like Amherst, ego-transcendence amounted to heresy because, as Buddha Mind, it recognizes no personal God.[25]

Her lonesome Glory was also a "strange Fame," because it was what she calls, in P-713, "Fame of Myself." This means what I call "intrapsychic fame," which is "strange" because it is esoteric. I first leaned about this when I read Lao Tzu.

The ***Tao Te Ching*** is a detailed discussion of how best to establish spiritual balance within by honoring our instinctual nature. The social ego-self must not be allowed to monopolize Psyche, as related in Chapter 17, Wu translation: "The highest type of ruler is one of whose existence the people are barely aware." Intrapsychically this means (in my version, ***The Yin–Yang Journal***),

---

25 Mystics of the traditional religions have always interpreted ego-transcendence in terms of a theology; like Gautama Buddha, ED would not take this route. Her skeptical temperament is one of her endearing qualities.

The best ego is one
of whose existence
Psyche is barely aware.

When Psyche (Mother Nature in human form) is liberated from ego-domination or repression, the creative energies flow. In ED's case, she became aware of her secret identity as Inspired Poet, & this was her inner fame. This surely impressed her as a strange realization! It is very strange indeed to recognize that you are not the person you were taught to be, that the ego-self has little to do with who you really are.

To me, the first line, "Gathered into the Earth," means "I was gathered into the Earth." Ego-transcendence awakened her instinctual nature & her true identity as Psyche, not as Emily Dickinson.

Gathered "out of story," she says. This is open to interpretation. In the context of transcendent experience I take "story" to mean "myth," since all mythology concerns transcendent truths intuited by ancient peoples closer to nature than to the modern ego-self.

Like us, ED lived in a thoroughly egocentric community. Her numinous experience of ego-transcendence gathered her being back into the world of Psyche, & seemed to be the very stuff of mythology come true. Emily Dickinson found that she had become ED-as-Psyche: a strange fame indeed, a mythological fame. To reveal it publicly would brand her as a lunatic; so for the rest of her life she made her poems, copied them out in a fair hand, stitched them into booklets, & stashed them. This is called Arts & Crafts. What a great hobby!

1589

Cosmopolites without a plea
Alight in every Land
The compliments of Paradise
From those within my Hand

Their dappled Journey to themselves
A compensation fair
Knock and it shall be opened
Is their Theology

1567

The Heart has many Doors –
I can but knock –
For any sweet "Come in"
Impelled to hark –
Not saddened by repulse,
Repast to me
That somewhere, there exists,
Supremacy –

317

Just so – Jesus – raps –
He – doesn't weary –
Last – at the Knocker –
And first – at the Bell.
Then – on divinest tiptoe – standing –
Might He but spy the lady's soul –
When He – retires –
Chilled – or weary –
It will be ample time for – me –
Patient – upon the steps – *until* then –
Heart! I am knocking – low at thee.

Ask, and it shall be given you; seek, and ye shall find; knock, and it shall be opened unto you."

—Matthew 7:7

THEOLOGY, THE SCIENCE OF GOD

ED came to understand that she was an American & a New Englander only fortuitously, because the higher Self transcends all such local identification. She was of the "ethereal throng" (P-1596), and the "imperial few" (P-1577) – the transcendentalists who have existed worldwide throughout history. In P-1589, cited here, she calls them Cosmopolites, "citizens of the world," or better yet, "citizens of the Cosmos."

To them she, as a fellow transcendentalist, sends her compliments, her cordial greetings, "From those within my Hand." These are greetings of solidarity based on her own many experiences of Paradise (this being a late poem). "Hand" may also refer to her large body of accumulated poems, copied out in her own hand & stashed away.

Each transcendentalist experiences a "dappled Journey," a checkered Path in life, marked by clustered days of light & darkness.

The Cosmopolites have no "plea," which I take in the legal sense (ED was fond of metaphorical legalese).[26] They have no plea, which is to say no plea of "innocent" or "guilty" regarding sin

26 See, for example, "affidavit" (poems 1180, 1228, 1408); "the Heavenly Clause" (P-1357); "patent" (P-1392, P-1744); "statutes do not meddle / With the internal bar" (P-1753); "God broke his contract to his Lamb" (P-1439); "Of Bliss the Codes are few" (P-1586).

or transgression against the Judge Upstairs. All their "theology" is summed up in the words of Christ: "Knock and it shall be opened" (line 7). Theology is the "science of God" in the old sense of "science," from L. *scio,* "I know." For the transcendentalist theology is the direct empirical knowledge of God, or Buddha Mind: unconditioned awareness.

The "knocking at the door" is clarified by the other two poems cited here, P-1567 & P-317. The last line of P-317 is the essence of ED's "theology": ego-transcendence occurs when the heart is sufficiently opened up, sufficiently awakened. It is what the Buddhists call bodhicitta, the awakened heart. As ED says in P-1567, "Somewhere (within the heart) there exists Supremacy." Supremacy is the enlightened awareness of the open heart, the "Supreme State," as Hindus call it.

1144

Ourselves we do inter with sweet derision.
The channel of the dust who once achieves
Invalidates the balm of that religion
That doubts as fervently as it believes.

992

The Dust behind I strove to join
Unto the Disk before –
But Sequence ravelled out of Sound
Like Balls upon a Floor –

937

I felt a Cleaving in my Mind –
As if my Brain had split –
I tried to match it – Seam by Seam –
But could not make them fit.

The thought behind, I strove to join
Unto the thought before –
But Sequence ravelled out of Sound
Like Balls – upon a Floor.

THE SEMANTICS OF EGO–TRANSCENDENCE

For the transcendentalist, consciousness is regularly experienced as twofold, a mingling of little self & Big Self – the everyday ego-identity & Higher Consciousness, Emily Dickinson & ED. Thus the pronouns with the suffix "-self" (myself, yourself, etc.) are always open to interpretation, & this is decided by context.

In P-1144 the first line, "Ourselves we do inter with sweet derision," may be read either conventionally or transcendentally. Conventionally it would have to refer to the funeral, in which case the adverbial phrase "with sweet derision" makes little sense. "We" don't bury people with "sweet derision." Nor can "Ourselves we do inter" be easily construed to mean "we bury the dead," or the questionable "we bury each other." In other words, an egocentric reading of this line yields no meaning. As a matter of fact, it is a good example of how egocentric readings & transcendental readings clash. Whenever a conventional reading seems meaningless or absurd, chances are that ED is composing a sutra, as it were.

The reader of an ED sutra/poem needs to bear in mind that for the transcendentalist, everyday life is an evolving dynamic between ego and non-ego – the so-called Individuation Process. If you are a committed vegetarian, every day you are aware that this is an ongoing fact of your life; if you are an awakened transcendentalist, then every day you think about it, for it is the largest fact in your life. Egocentric people are not aware of any "self" beyond the ego-identity, & if they read Emily Dickinson they are not aware of ED. They may be ordinary readers, or they may be scholars; in either case Miss Emily's cryptic poetry puzzles them. For the egocentric reader transcendentalist discourse is a sealed book. In fact, ***this confirms what ED says right here***: "Ourselves we do inter with sweet derision."

Everyone has a true Self & a false self. Ego-identity, the false self, is taught to repress – bury, "inter" – the true Self "with sweet derision" (e.g., "yogis contemplate their bellybutton").

Line 2 says, "The channel of the dust who once achieves." The person "who once achieves" is the enlightened one, the one who has achieved satori. To understand "dust," we may recall that elsewhere ED uses "dust" to mean the everyday, conventional self. In P-1527 she refers to "that Pink stranger we call Dust." P-1539, ED's version of the child's bedtime prayer, says

> Now I lay thee down to Sleep –
> I pray the Lord thy Dust to keep –

P-992, the second poem above, is about the duality of little self & Big Self. When ego-transcendence happens, you "leave the Dust behind." (P-992 is a variant of P-937, which has more detail.)

The "high achiever" leaves behind a Path, a "channel of dust," leading to the awakened certainty of Buddha Mind. It is this that "invalidates the balm" of our religions. The intensely secular American society may profess to be Christian, but it clearly "doubts as fervently as it believes" – nay, more fervently, because most Americans do not live in the Bible Belt.

827

The Only News I know
Is Bulletins all Day
From Immortality.

The Only Shows I see –
Tomorrow and Today –
Perchance Eternity –

The Only One I meet
Is God – The Only Street –
Existence – This traversed

If Other News there be –
Or Admirabler Show –
I'll tell it You –

> In the United States, ninety-nine percent of all homes have a TV set, and the average person watches nearly four hours per day.
>
> *Shift* (March-May 2004, p.11)

TRANSCENDENTAL TELEVISION

If you were to ask ED, "Do you watch TV?" this poem is the answer you would get. Couch potatoes watch "shows" & "the news"; so does ED, except that she watches different shows & different news.

News bulletins tell us what is going on right now in the world. In ED's own everyday life, Now is what is going on Right Now: "Flash! The Now Moment is currently in progress!"

In Buddhist writings the Now Moment is sometimes likened to the ***bardos*** of the Tibetan Book of the Dead. The bardos are the in-between stages that one passes through between death & reincarnation.

This idea of the In-Between is applied to every moment in one's own life, every moment of breathing in & breathing out. In Breathing Meditation you concentrate on this. Each breath is transient, & there is a bardo between each inbreath & outbreath. This bardo is pregnant with rebirth: at any moment you can be reborn, i.e., enlightened. As ED says in this poem, between Today & Tomorrow, Eternity may be born. She knows this from personal experience.

Her use of "show" has a double meaning. It means both "entertainment," & "empirical evidence" (cf. Missouri, the "Show-me State"). The only existential evidence acceptable to ED is empirical.

She says, "The Only One I meet / is God." If you think of "God" as her term for Buddha Mind, then of course it follows that it is the "Only One," since it is nondual awareness. Ultimately Reality is One, not two.

The only Path (or "Street") in life is the Path of Existence. As ED says, you "traverse" this path, meaning that you go from here to there – from dual mind to the Only One.

In each poem ED writes she is telling us something about the nature of human life/consciousness. This is her calling, to be our News Reporter; if anything "Admirabler" turns up, she'll be the first to let us know.[27]

---

27 "Admirabler" is a typical ED comparative. Some examples: "contenteder," "consciouser" (P-762), "passiver" (652), "supremer" (232), "terribler" (244), "infiniter" (625), excellenter" (968), fruitlesser" (926), etc. It is one of her ways of making us pay attention. (Thoreau also used "news" as a metaphor for Awakening: he said, "Don't read the *Times*, read the Eternities.")

THE FOUR NOBLE TRUTHS

When Gautama Buddha awoke he understood four basic things, now called the Four Noble Truths: (1) life is suffering, (2) suffering is caused by attachment, (3) liberation from suffering is bliss, & (4) liberation may be attained through meditation & right conduct.

The Buddha did not "formulate" these statements in the way that a scientist may formulate a theory; he awoke to inevitable truths that he himself had experienced, as did ED, whose written record restates these truths in many & varied ways.

1. LIFE IS SUFFERING

1168

As old as Woe –
How old is that?
Some eighteen thousand years –
As old as Bliss
How old is that
They are of equal years

Together chiefest they are found
But seldom side by side
From neither of then tho' he try
Can Human nature hide

SUFFERING & BLISS

ED's awakening revealed that suffering & enlightenment are the two qualities essential to the human condition: they are as old as consciousness, "Some eighteen thousand years," i.e., since the dawn of human awareness.[28]

In this poem ED uses the question/answer format, like a disciple asking questions of the teacher: "What does ***old*** mean?" "It means ***enduring,*** as human consciousness down through the ages."

This age-old experience of human awareness is informed by two essential qualities, Suffering & Bliss.

Suffering & bliss are not typically found "side by side," for Woe is the essence of ego-life, & Bliss is the essence of non-ego life. Ultimately human nature cannot hide from either, even though "he" try.[29] Enlightenment reveals what had to happen eventually: you have been liberated from the essence of egocentric life – suffering.

---

28 Cf. Lao Tzu's use of "the 10,000 things" (myriad), meaning "countless."

29 Common usage for ED ("he" instead of "it"). Cf. P-316 (wind), P-429 (sea), P-748 (autumn), P-909 (moon), P-1291 (desert), P-1316 (winter), P-1400 (grass), etc.

405

It might be lonelier
Without the Loneliness –
I'm so accustomed to my Fate –
Perhaps the Other – Peace –

Would interrupt the Dark –
And crowd the little Room –
Too scant – by Cubits – to contain
The Sacrament - of Him –

I am not used to Hope –
It might intrude upon –
Its sweet parade – blaspheme the place –
Ordained to Suffering –

It might be easier
To fail – with Land in Sight –
Than gain – My Blue Peninsula –
To perish – of Delight –

EGO–SELF: THE PLACE ORDAINED TO SUFFERING

Here Emily Dickinson speaks in the ego-dominant mode, "the place - / Ordained to Suffering." Spoken like a Buddhist reciting the First Noble Truth! Robert Thurman, one of the veteran leaders of the American Buddhist Movement, describes the hopelessness of the ego-bound, ego-fixated life:

> Most of us have a strong yet unwarranted sense of having a fixed, unchanging, limited "self" that is totally separate from all other beings. This combines with our narrow view that our existence is random and terminal... Fixed and alienated, random and terminal – together these form a vicious combination. In the end, we are left feeling bereft and slightly depressed, living a life seeming to be utterly devoid of meaning. I call this "terminal Living."[30]

In P-405, line 3, Emily Dickinson says, "I'm so accustomed to my Fate." Everyone has a lower "fate" & a Higher Fate, of course. In the present poem Dickinson refers to the lonely fate of living apart from ED, not knowing if ED will ever again return. Once you have experienced the liberation of the awakened Buddha Mind, the fixated ego-identity seems like a prison, a Dark Night of the Soul.

Dickinson's use of "blaspheme" in line 11 turns the meaning of this word on its head. "Blaspheme" means "to speak irreverently of God"; here (just after mentioning "The Sacrament – of

30 *Infinite Life*, xix-xx.

Him" (i.e. Buddha Mind), she speaks of blaspheming "the place – Ordained to Suffering."

This place is the ego, recognized as the basic reality of everyday life. American culture worships ego, & exalts its celebrities in show biz & professional sports.[31] Hoping for ego-transcendence blasphemes the Great God Ego.

---

31 Ironically, Robert Thurman, veteran Buddhist leader & longtime friend of the Dalai Lama, is the father of a currently much admired actress, Uma Thurman. (*Uma* is a spiral or tuft of hair between the eyebrows, one of the "marks" [*laksana*] of the Buddha.)

910

Experience is the Angled Road
Preferred against the Mind
By – Paradox – the Mind itself –
Presuming it to lead

Quite Opposite – How Complicate
The Discipline of Man –
Compelling Him to Choose Himself
His Preappointed Pain –

EGO-SELF: THE PREAPPOINTED PAIN

Speaking of her own experience (as usual) ED calls it an "Angled Road." "Angled" means "placed at an angle to something else" (Oxford Dictionary). This "something else" is what we might call one's "normal life." The experience of waking up as ED was at an angle to Emily Dickinson's quiet life in everyday Amherst.

ED says that this experience is "Preferred against the Mind," paradoxically "the Mind itself." This paradox is resolved by considering that for the transcendentalist, whether ED or Gautama Buddha, there are two minds in every human being. This is the nature of human consciousness. There is dual mind (the ego-identity) & there is nondual mind (non-ego awareness). Nondual mind is Buddha Mind, i.e., "awakened" mind. Emily Dickinson & ED led a paradoxical dual existence that she called "mutual Monarch" in P-642:

> But since Myself – assault Me –
> How have I peace
> Except by subjugating
> Consciousness?
>
> And since We're mutual Monarch
> How this be
> Except by Abdication
> Me – of Me?

Emily Dickinson & ED traded back & forth, but were not felt to be two different people, not "monarchs," but "monarch." This is the mystery, like God the Father & the Son being different but identical. The first stanza of the present poem may be paraphrased:

> ED Experience is the Angled Road
> Preferred against ego-mind,
> paradoxically Big Mind itself,
> presuming it to lead.

Emily Dickinson "presumes" – takes it for granted – that ED is her leader in the life of Psyche.

In the second stanza ED contrasts her own case with that of egocentric people. It is "Quite Opposite." The "Discipline of Man" is the behavior in accord with the rules of conduct: the good citizen is disciplined to identify with the collective mind & to live accordingly.

But egocentric life is ultimately pain (duhkha), as the First Noble Truth says. It is doomed to be so – or, as ED puts it, it is a "Preappointed Pain."

The egocentric life is "complicate(d)" by contrast with the simplicity of nondual mind. Every egocentric person is compelled (as it were) to embrace his or her pain of preference; living an egocentric life compels you to "name your poison."

572

Delight – becomes pictorial –
When viewed through Pain –
More fair – because impossible
That any gain –

The Mountain – at a given distance –
In Amber – lies –
Approached – the Amber flits – a little –
And That's – the Skies –

EGO-SELF: BORN TO SUFFER

"Suffering" is a common translation of the Sanskrit ***duhkha,*** also translated as "unsatisfactoriness." Zen priest Steve Hagen explains duhkha as originally referring to a wheel out of kilter. It causes a vehicle to wobble, like an annoying shopping cart.

> The first truth...likens human life to this out-of-kilter wheel. Something basic and important isn't right. It bothers us, makes us unhappy, time after time. With each turn of the wheel, each passing day, we experience pain.[32]

The basis of the problem is the ego-identity, of course, which all meditators, Buddhist & otherwise, seek to transcend. Dual mind – "ego" vs. "world" – lives alone & separate, & thinks to find its place on earth through attachments – hence the Second Noble Truth: "duhkha is caused by attachment, or desire." Even pleasure itself is duhkha, since it is ego's fruitless attempt to be "happy."

Any ego-experience of delight or happiness is therefore limited by the limitations of ego itself. It falls short of the ideal as enshrined in the portrayals of beauty by the old masters (or the new). To view happiness through the lens of the ego-self is to view it "through Pain," as ED says here:

> Delight – becomes pictorial –
> When viewed through Pain –

32 ***Buddhism Plain and Simple,*** 26.

Its fullness remains distant, like a beautiful landscape, unattainable because ego-limitations preclude any generous or big-hearted approach, or full immersion. Genuine ecstasy requires ego-loss. Without this, beauty remains hazy, at a distance, like a mountain on the horizon, bathed "In Amber." But the mountain, when actually approached without the tether of ego, is the "Ancestor of Dawn" (P-975): "And That's – the Skies" – the clarity of your original Face.

It has not occurred to any Dickinson commentator (so far as I know) that ***the source of ED's unhappiness was ego-identity itself,*** a violation of her own original sense of who she was & is. The egocentric reader will naturally suppose that ED's problems were "ego-problems," not "problems with ego." Here is a typical comment:

> Whatever emotional disaster it was that drove her to elect and finally covet a life of obscurity, poetry was the thing that made that life tolerable and transformed it into a creative career.[33]

This is like saying that poetry made life tolerable for St. John of the Cross, or that painting made life tolerable for El Greco. Or that keeping a log makes life tolerable for the sea captain.

The transcendentalist reader can immediately understand the problem of viewing pleasure through the duhkha of ego. This is the viewpoint of all serious Buddhist meditators. ED had this problem as she says in a late poem (1741): "Believing what we don't believe / Does not exhilarate." Trying to make it through life with an unreal ego-identity means "believing what you don't believe." Any gay teenager will tell you that this does not exhilarate!

---

33 John Malcolm Brinnin, ***Emily Dickinson***, 13.

1261

A Word dropped careless on a Page
May stimulate an eye
When folded in perpetual seam
The Wrinkled Maker lie

Infection in the sentence breeds
We may inhale Despair
At distances of Centuries
From the Malaria –

A FEBRILE INFECTION

Even the most casually written words, as in informal letters, if saved or archived, can carry an emotion down through the centuries (as many a document from ancient Rome or China). If the writer has captured in language his or her own suffering, its contagion can spread timelessly from reader to reader.

That is what the present poem states. It is a truism, interesting, but not especially original. What I find of special interest is the example which ED adduces: despair or suffering. She could have chosen laughter as her example, for is not laughter contagious?

But the two basic modes of tragedy & comedy have a special relationship in transcendentalist psychology, as we have seen in our discussion of P-1168 ("As old as Woe"). There we noted that woe, or suffering, is the essence of egocentric life, while Bliss is the essence of Enlightenment. While happiness is frequently found in egocentric life, it is not essential to it; suffering ***is***, however, as the First Noble Truth declares. Suffering is inevitable; happiness is not.

Despair (line 6) is, according to Christian teaching, the most serious of the mortal sins (it is the lowest circle of Dante's Inferno). Despair is the loss of hope that one may ever see God.

But it is the ego-self who despairs, the one who loses religious faith. This reveals the abyss separating Christianity & Buddhism: the Buddhist seeks to transcend the ego-self, whereas the Christian seeks to glorify it. What the Buddhist calls Bliss, or Nirvana ("extinction of ego") is regarded by the Christian ego-self as a catastrophe.

In the present poem ED chooses Despair as her example of

what is essential to the heritage of egocentric people, passed on down from generation to generation. This is the Egocentric Transmission; egocentrism is a feverish infection.

2. SUFFERING IS CAUSED BY ATTACHMENT

1040

Not so the infinite Relations – Below
Division is Adhesion's forfeit – On High
Affliction but a Speculation – And Woe
A Fallacy, a Figment, We knew –

ADHESION'S FORFEIT

ED contrasts ego-mind ("Below") with non-ego mind ("On High"). She begins her discourse in medias res, without preamble. After ego-transcendence, she says, you see clearly that the infinite Relations are "not so," not like our everyday finite relations. You come down from the "high," look around with new eyes, & say, "How I always have been seeing this world is not so!"

Down here below, "Division is Adhesion's forfeit."

"Adhesion" is what the Buddha called "clinging." A basic teaching of his, much quoted by Buddhist teachers, says, "Nothing whatsoever should be clung to as 'I' or 'mine.'" When you become attached to anything, then you create a duality: I crave that, I need you. This is the cause of duhkha, "suffering," or "unsatisfactoriness."

Suffering – "Affliction" in the present poem – is here seen to be "but a Speculation," a conjecture that it is real, without any factual basis. "Woe" is an illusion, because ego is an illusion. As one roshi put it, "no ego, no problem."

ED "ends" this poem much as she began it, with an implied context: "We knew," meaning perhaps, a woe we once regarded as real, now seen to be a fallacy. This is true of her early experience of ego-transcendence, "woefully" regarded as madness.

669

No Romance sold unto
Could so enthrall a Man
As the perusal of
His Individual One –
'Tis Fiction's – to dilute to Plausibility
Our Novel – When 'tis small enough
To Credit – 'Tisn't true!

BESTSELLER

This poem is one of ED's clearest statements concerning the unreality of the social self, the ego-identity. One may be "enthralled" reading a romance – in our days romance novels – but there is no more enthralling fiction than our own ego, our "Individual One." This is "***Our*** Novel" (line 6). As usual, the role of fiction is to "dilute to Plausibility" to stay within the bounds of the reader's belief, to allow for suspension of disbelief.

But the ego-self, small or large, is always a fiction. When ego is "small enough / To Credit," even then "'Tisn't true!" (last line). Ego-transcendence does not allow for any ontological suspension of disbelief. Even the most modest of egos cannot pass itself off as nonfiction. Buddhists recognize that we all spend most of out time lost in our life "story." Joseph Goldstein, one of the elders of American Buddhism, compares the ego-self to cinema:

> ...we go to the movies and become totally absorbed in the film. Then there is a moment when we step out of the theater and experience that sudden reality shift, a mini-awakening to where we really are. In the same way we are often lost in the movies of our mind. ...the biggest story, the most fundamental story, is the idea of self.[34]

ED cannily uses the word "enthrall," for it means not only "to charm," but also "to captivate, to enslave": a thrall is a slave, after all. (In P-1740 she vividly describes the flight of panic as an "enthralling gallop").

---

34 *Tricycle* (Winter, 1993), 13.

They call it "socialization," teaching children how to develop a socially acceptable "Individual One." This is at best an acceptable fiction (even the Dalai Lama needs a functioning ego-self), a fact taught by the Individuation Process, whereby we gradually become the *real* Individual One – "Individual" meaning "unique" – that we were born to be.

594

The Battle fought between the Soul
And No Man – is the One
Of all the Battles prevalent –
By far the Greater One –

No News of it is had abroad –
Its Bodiless Campaign
Establishes, and terminates –
Invisible – Unknown –

Nor History – record it –
As Legions of a Night
The Sunrise scatters – These endure –
Enact – and terminate –

AN AMERICAN CIVIL WAR

ED was in her thirties at the time of the American Civil War, & she was clearly impressed by the fact that the great event defining her own life was precisely an internal civil war. She describes this in P-642:

> Me from Myself – to banish –
> Had I Art –
> Impregnable my Fortress
> Unto All Heart –
>
> But since Myself – assault Me –
> How have I peace
> Except by subjugating
> Consciousness?
>
> And since We're mutual Monarch
> How this be
> Except by Abdication –
> Me – of Me?

Emily Dickinson & ED are two "mutual monarch(s)," incompatible, & so engaged in a great civil war, testing who shall long endure. The Individuation Process unleashes a war between ego & non-ego, between the ego-self & Psyche, our instinctual Nature. The extraordinary power of ego nearly always monopolizes Psyche, like an efficient dictator; little wonder that Lao Tzu, in the *Tao Te Ching,* envisioned the Individuation Process as a military undertaking. ED recognized this civil war as the greatest event that could occur in the evolution of Psyche; in P-822 she calls it the "most profound experiment [experience] / Appointed unto Men." In the present poem she calls it

> Of all the Battles prevalent
> By far the Greater One –

Such is the "Battle fought between the Soul / And No Man," i.e., between two elements within the soul. It is a spiritual war, a "Bodiless Campaign." It

> Establishes, and terminates –
> Invisible – Unknown –

Ideally it will abolish slavery to ego-attachment & emancipate the Self. The ego-self is what ED recognizes as the "Invisible Unknown." All serious meditators quickly become aware of this signal fact about one's own ego. Until you attempt to vanquish it, you have no idea of its power, hidden until defied; then it begins to manifest as an Invisible Unknown. Buddhist teacher Ted Rose describes this vividly:

> So I planned a retreat. I did it in 1972 at Karmê Chöling. I didn't know what to expect. I had visions of peace and solitude and quiet and tranquility. During the first week I discovered that I had the most agitated, chaotic, neurotic mind that I could have possibly imagined. My mind was insane. After one week, I couldn't take it anymore, sitting in that little cabin hour after hour. I said, "I'm sorry, I just cannot do this." I made myself stay until the end of the week, and then I left. Actually, I left in the middle of the night, running down the hill in the dead of winter in my bedroom

> slippers and pajamas. I had to get out of there. That was my first experience.[35]

ED says that "no news" of this struggle "is had abroad," nor does "History – record it." It is an internal battle fought by Armies of the Night, so to speak. The sun rises & sets daily, & no one the wiser. ED's family & friends remained unaware of her lifelong secret war recorded in booklets hidden away. It is in those booklets where it all "endures" – takes place & runs its course. (P-1549: "My Wars are laid away in Books").

When I read here, "No News of it is had abroad," I think that what I now write & publish about ED's poetry is the News Going Abroad at last, more than a century later.

---

35 *Tricycle*, (Spring, 2005), 41.

ADDENDUM

After writing the above commentary, I came across an extraordinary statement written by an egocentric scholar, denying everything ED says about "The Battle fought between the Soul / And No Man." It demonstrates ego's ability to repress Buddha Mind in favor of its own ontology. The author, David Brion Davis, is writing about the history of American slavery, but oddly, he begins with a gratuitous remark about non-ego reality:

> I have long believed that what most distinguishes us from all other animals is our ability to transcend an illusory sense of *now*, of an eternal present, and to strive for an understanding of the forces and events that made us what we are. Such an understanding seems to me the prerequisite for all human freedom.[36]

Transcendentalists know that "what most distinguishes us from all other animals" is precisely our ability to transcend the illusory sense of a "substantial" ego-self. They know this because ego-transcendence awakens one from immersion in the fantasy of the collective ego that says, "We think, therefore we are."

There is no evidence that "all other animals" possess a "sense" of *now*, because they have no ego-self to transcend in order to realize a new mode of consciousness. The human being is the only animal able to do these two things: (1) create an ego-self, & (2) transcend it. Lao Tzu, in the ***Tao Te Ching***, has thought about egocentric scholars, & has come to this conclusion:

---

36 *American Heritage*(Feb/March, 2005), 65.

When a wise scholar hears the Tao,
He practices it diligently.
When a mediocre scholar hears the Tao,
He wavers between belief and unbelief.
When a worthless scholar hears the Tao,
He laughs boisterously at it.
But if such a one does not laugh at it,
The Tao would not be the Tao!

(*#41*, Wu translation)

The idea here is that ego-transcendence – satori – is its own validation; but in order for this to be so, ***there must be an ego to transcend.*** ED valued Emily Dickinson, because without Emily Dickinson, ED could never have come into being.

Ironically, Davis' field of study is human slavery – but it has not occurred to him the Psyche is enslaved by ego. "Human freedom" does not consist in understanding history, but rather in experiencing liberation, as the Zen koan has been demonstrating for centuries.

1242

To flee from memory
Had we the Wings
Many would fly
Inured to slower things
Birds with surprise
Would scan the cowering Van
Of men escaping
From the mind of man

IF I HAD THE WINGS OF AN ANGEL

This poem evokes the prison folksong that says,

> Oh, if I had the wings of an angel
> over these prison walls I would fly

Transcendentalists think of the ego-self as a kind of prison, & this is a theme in the poetry of ED, as in the early P-77:

> I never hear the word "escape"
> Without a quicker blood,
> A sudden expectation,
> A flying attitude!
>
> I never hear of prisons broad
> By soldiers battered down,
> But I tug childish at my bars
> Only to fail again!

In the present poem she says that if "we" – human beings – could fly over these prison walls, many would fly away so fast that it would surprise even the birds, who are "Inured to slower things."

This poem is epigrammatic, meaning that each word is carefully chosen. "Many" (line 3) is such a word. If human beings had the power to transcend memory (she says), "many" would take advantage; not everyone, yet "many." This is a relative term, & may mean "a majority," or "a large minority" (as when we say that in our town there are "many" gay people). In this sense "many" means "more than you would expect."

ED defines her terms. "To flee from memory" means "to escape from the mind of man" (last line). By this I understand "each person's ego-self." This "mind" regards itself as a substantial reality; ***it is attached to itself.*** This attachment is entirely dependent upon memory, & this illusion of continuity is the source of needless suffering, of duhkha, "unsatisfactoriness."

If people knew that they could transcend this prison, "many" would do so, so fast it would make your head spin. But most people, committed to the prison of the ego-self, do not feel any need to flee. As ED says in P-652, "A Prison gets to be a friend." People take pride in the "nobility" of ego-suffering, & admire tragic heroes. The transcendentalist, however, is one who cannot relate to ego's high regard for itself as a noble sufferer.

1331

Wonder – is not precisely Knowing
And not precisely Knowing not –
A beautiful but bleak condition
He has not lived who has not felt –

Suspense – is his maturer Sister –
Whether Adult Delight is Pain
Or of itself a new misgiving –
This is the Gnat that mangles men –

EGO-ATTACHMENT, THE GNAT THAT MANGLES MEN

There are two forms of ***wonder***: egocentric & ego-transcendent. The first is akin to curiosity, even idle curiosity; the second means "reverent awe." Since the present poem is concerned with defining "wonder," I believe that it necessarily refers to ego-transcendence, since this was the great wonder of ED's life. Not only that; she calls it "A beautiful but bleak condition," which sounds like a reference to the Dark Night of the Soul.

ED wonders not only at the fact of ego-transcendence, but at the future possibility of its recurrence. This, clearly, is not mere curiosity or speculation. It is, as she says in line 5, "Suspense," for it keeps her suspended between Heaven & Earth. It is somewhere between knowing & not knowing. Suspense is the "maturer Sister" of Wonder (ego-transcendence), because they come from the same womb. Ego-transcendence cannot happen without making you wonder if it will ever happen again, & this induces into your life a high suspense.

"Adult Delight" (line 6) is mature, full-grown Bliss, admixed with a lot of pain & misgiving for someone isolated in a nineteenth-century American village, with no sangha, or support group, to share the experience. ED's isolation certainly must have contributed to periodic misgivings; the fact that she had to find her own inner guru, & had to stay the course for her entire life, required a heroic commitment. Her poetic genius made it possible, just as ego-transcendence made possible her poetic genius. This dynamic reciprocity was never far from her mind, as is evident in P-642, the "mutual Monarch" poem.

ED caps her definition of "wonder" by calling it "the Gnat that mangles men." In poems 534 & 641 the gnat is contrasted to the giant, just as ego contrasts to Buddha Mind. In P-534 the ego-self is a "Gnat's embrace"; in P-641

> The Giant tolerates no Gnat
> For ease of Gianture –

In that same poem ED goes on to say that the "intrinsic size" of the Giant (non-ego mind)

> Ignores the possibility
> Of Calumnies – or Flies.

ED was certainly aware that she was "calumniated" as the village weirdo, & that the town gossips were like flies & gnats picking at her public image as the daughter of a prominent family. But her own ego-self was the first of these "gnats," assaulting her with misgivings. To the transcendentalist the ego-self is a mere gnat – but it is the gnat that "mangles men" – nay, it is the story of civilization, the story of the ancient Greeks' tragic hero. For all its intrinsic size, Buddha Mind, for most Westerners, appears to be virtually defenseless against the repressive powers of the ego-self.

700

You've seen Balloons set – Haven't You?
So stately they ascend –
It is as Swans – discarded You,
For Duties Diamond –

Their Liquid Feet go softly out
Upon a Sea of Blonde –
They spurn the Air, as 'twere too mean
For Creatures so renowned –

Their Ribbons just beyond the eye –
They struggle – some – for Breath –
And yet the Crowd applaud, below –
They would not encore – Death –

The Gilded Creature strains – and spins –
Trips frantic in a Tree –
Tears open her imperial Veins –
And tumbles in the Sea –

The Crowd – retire with an Oath –
The Dust in Streets – go down –
And Clerks in Counting Rooms
Observe – "'Twas only a Balloon" –

THE POWER OF EGO-ATTACHMENT

> Q. Can people have a genuine awakening and not be aware that they're awake?
>
> A. It's common for people to have a deep seeing of truth and then to throw it out because it doesn't fit their preconceptions.[37]

The above remark has great relevance to ED's life in Amherst. From the time she first began to have a "deep seeing of truth," she treasured it as if she had stumbled across a gold mine. Early on she was troubled by the idea that she might be crazy, but she soon got beyond that.

Adyashanti's remark quoted above is easily understood in terms of our dream life. Probably everyone has had at least one numinous dream over the years, but in the West the common reaction to this reflects the last line of the present poem: "'Twas only a dream."

Like any other transcendentalist ED felt a spiritual connection with the flight of birds – & of balloons. These rise, free of the earth-bound obsessions of the ego-identity. After all, enlightenment has always been referred to as "liberation." In modern times the hot-air balloon is a natural archetype for liberation from dual ego-mind's attachment to itself. In P-1118 ED describes this "Exhilaration":

---

37 Adyashanti, Zen-trained lay teacher, in ***Tricycle***, (Fall, 2004), 110.

Exhilaration is the Breeze
That lifts us from the Ground
And leaves us in another place
Whose statement is not found –

Returns us not, but after time
We soberly descend
A little newer for the term
Upon Enchanted Ground –

In P-1630 the balloon is likened to the transcendentalist temperament, which (like that of the Buddhist meditator) seeks "nothing but release":

As from the earth the light Balloon
Asks nothing but release –
Ascension that for which it was,
Its soaring Residence.
The spirit looks upon the Dust
That fastened it so long
With indignation,
As a Bird
Defrauded of its song.

ED's main thought in the present poem is about the setting of balloons, not their rising: "You've seen Balloons set – Haven't You?" Given her own experience, she is very aware of how people typically react to the "setting" of a balloon, especially a crash. I say "people," meaning what ED here calls "The Crowd." She is no doubt describing an event that she witnessed, & could not help but be impressed by people's "rush to judgment": "'Twas only a Balloon." What goes up must come down, including Icarus.

This was the story of her life. When she first awakened, she did not say, "'Twas only a Balloon." She said, "'Twas nothing less than a Balloon!" In P-1348 ED completes the thought of how one is to assess the advent of awakening. First, we must not dismiss it; second, we have an obligation to bear witness:

> Lift it – with the Feathers
> Not alone we fly –
> Launch it – the aquatic
> Not the only sea –
> Advocate the Azure
> To the lower Eyes –
> He has obligation
> Who has Paradise –

This is the thought embraced by the transcendentalists: first, you honor the experience of awakening; second, you share it with the world just as Gautama Buddha did. Certainly ED was attached to the ego-self; this underlies all the struggle & drama between the "Mutual Monarch(s)" (P-642). But the power of her Enlightenment impressed upon her mind the impossibility of returning to the "Counting Rooms," observing cynically, "'Twas only a Balloon."

753

My Soul – accused me – And I quailed –
As Tongues of Diamond had reviled
All else accused me – and I smiled –
My Soul – that Morning – was My friend –

Her favor – is the best Disdain
Toward Artifice of Time – or Men –
But Her Disdain – 'twere lighter bear
A finger of Enamelled Fire –

Indict. To accuse of wrongdoing.

(Random House Dictionary)

VALID INDICTMENT, INVALID INDICTMENT

This poem concerns the Spirit facing two different forms of "accusation," inner & outer. You may feel yourself "accused" by others, as in the form of social disapproval; or you may feel yourself "accused" by your own inner Self. Reducing this to a basic conflict of interest, we may say that ED, as a loner, recognized that her reclusiveness earned social disapproval; at the same time, any willingness to compromise her psychic integrity – Oneness with heart & mind – would stir up a well-deserved inner disapproval.

Hence the present poem says, in effect, "When my Soul accused me of betraying my spiritual commitment to the Higher Self, I quailed. I took it very seriously, & I recognized that my Soul was my Friend.

"When society disapproved of my aloofness, I merely smiled."

When the inner spirit favors you, it confirms your "Disdain / Toward Artifice of Time – or Men." This evokes P-970:

> Color – Caste – Denomination –
> These – are Time's Affair –

Ego-transcendent values disdain egocentric artifices. This "corrective disdain" is a tough challenge, hard to bear. I take the last two lines to mean that it would be easier to bear "A finger of

Enamelled Fire," than to bear the Spirit accusing you of betrayal. The image suggests a form of exquisite torture that ED cannot abide. It is like the "awe" of P-1678

> That searches Human Nature's creases
> As clean as Fire.

Thus ED articulates the inner balance of power that was constantly changing in the struggle between what she calls in P-642, the "mutual Monarch(s)." In the long run, the inner Spirit of the transcendentalist will rebel against attempts to form ego-attachments. It is fine to have loving relationships with family & friends, but they must not become a form of ego-attachment; if they do, then you have learned nothing from the great gift of ego-transcendence.

1299

Delight's Despair at setting
Is that Delight is less
Than the sufficing Longing
That so impoverish.

Enchantment's Perihelion
Mistaken oft has been
For the Authentic orbit
Of its Anterior Sun.

> Perihelion. The point in the orbit of a planet…at which it is nearest to the sun.
>
> (Random House Dictionary)

LESSER & GREATER BLISS

Like P-934 ("That is solemn we have ended"), the present poem is a meditation on the suffering caused by ego-attachment to transient objects: with their passing, Delight turns to Despair. ED explains that our longing suffices to create happiness when it is realized – but then our resultant happiness proves to be less than the longing.

The greatest joy possible is the Bliss of Buddha Mind, which is like the Sun itself, where "Consciousness – is Noon" (P-1056). Egocentric happiness, no matter how intense, by comparison with Bliss, is a "Perihelion" (Gk. *Peri-* + *helios*, "around the sun"). ED says that Enchantment's Perihelion has "often" been mistaken "For the Authentic orbit / Of its Anterior Sun."

"Enchantment" (line 5) may be either egocentric or ego-transcendent (for the latter, see poems 838, 1118, 1451); in the present poem ED is speaking of a kind of egocentric enchantment which has "often" been mistaken for the real thing. I can think of two basic kinds of "pseudo-Bliss" which approach the real thing so closely that they are not only "often," but "typically" mistaken for the Bliss of Buddha Mind: these are (1) Romantic love, & (2) religious ecstasy (as at the revival meetings popular during ED's time).

Romantic love, as experienced by the great Romantic poets &

composers of Europe, attains ecstatic heights – but it remains essentially an egocentric form of mutual attachment between two people.[38]

The religious ecstasy, as of the charismatic churches, is rooted in the theistic idea of a savior: if you can muster sufficient blind-faith energy, the Man Upstairs will save your soul. But as ED, the transcendentalist, says in P-1347, when she escapes from the egocentric mode, "'Tis not to sight the savior - / It is to be the saved." One's salvation is up to the individual, as the Buddha himself understood "salvation":

> In his own time, the Buddha set accepted wisdom on its ear by insisting that liberation was a personal responsibility, independent of birth, priestly intervention, or ritual performance...[39]

When the people at a revival meeting rise up in ecstasy, they are mistaking their sectarian bliss for that of the "Anterior Sun," the Bliss that necessarily antedates any theological tinkering.

---

38 The Romantic poets are patriarchal, & see the woman as their *anima*, something to "complete" them. Traditional Tantric Buddhism seeks non-ego Bliss through the cultivation of erotic love between man & woman in a fully equal relationship.

39 Kate Wheeler, *Tricycle* (Summer, 1994), 87.

3. LIBERATION FROM SUFFERING IS BLISS

273

He put the Belt around my life –
I heard the Buckle snap –
And turned away, imperial,
My Lifetime folding up –
Deliberate, as a Duke would do
A Kingdom's Title Deed –
Henceforth, a Dedicated sort –
A Member of the Cloud.

Yet not too far to come at call –
And do the little Toils
That make the Circuit of the Rest –
And deal occasional smiles
To lives that stoop to notice mine –
And kindly ask it in –
Whose invitation, know you not
For Whom I must decline?

BUCKLING UP

This is an early poem in which ED attempts to deal with the dilemma posed by ego-transcendence. She could not devote herself entirely to the transcendent life nor to the everyday, egocentric life. Her vocation was that of witness/poet, & she devoted herself to this with great constancy all her life, as stated in P-750:

> Effort – is the sole condition –
> Patience of Itself –
> Patience of opposing forces –
> And intact Belief –

Our understanding of the present poem depends upon our reading of "my life," in the opening line. I take it to mean the everyday life of Emily Dickinson, by contrast with the transcendent life of ED (just as we distinguish between the ego-self of Mohandas Karamchand Gandhi & the Higher Self of Mahatma.)

"He" clearly refers to ego-transcendent mind (God Mind or Buddha Mind), experienced as an entity beyond the narrow limits of the profane ego-identity. The latter got "folded up," secured within a "Circuit" of daily activity (line 11), what she calls a "Demurer Circuit" in P-652 ("A Prison gets to be a friend"). It is as if Buddha Mind set very definite limits to the amount of life energy she could afford to spend as Emily Dickinson, expressed in the image of packing something in a suitcase for indefinite storage – "self storage," to borrow a modern term.[40] The "Title

40 I think of her hidden stash of transcendental poetry as her Self-storage.

Deed" to her life was appropriated – confiscated, if you like – by imperial decree.

ED commonly uses the metaphor of royalty to name the transcendent state – Queen, Majesty, Sire, King, Empress, etc. – & here

Deliberate, as a Duke would do
A Kingdom's Title Deed –

In P-466 ("'Tis little I – could care for Pearls") she calls herself "the Prince of Mines." Buddha Mind, whom she addresses as "Sire," "Master," "Lord," etc., is simply her Higher Self, the Inner Guru recognized by Buddhist adepts. When the Inner Guru packed away her egocentric life – put it on the back burner, so to speak – she became

Henceforth, a Dedicated sort –
A Member of the Cloud.

This makes her a member of the "imperial few" (P-1577), of the "ethereal throng" (P-1596).

It is helpful to point out here how ED uses "buckle" elsewhere. In P-1748 she describes how volcanoes give no warning:

The reticent volcano keeps
His never slumbering plan –
Confided are his projects pink
To no precarious man.

For ED the volcano was a symbol of her own creative self periodically erupting (P-1677), & in this later volcano poem she says,

Admonished by her buckled lips
Let every babbler be

So "buckle" is a metaphor for suppression or repression (today we say, "My lips are sealed").

ED endeavored to carry on a dual life, though eventually Emily Dickinson was given precious little energy to be very meaningful. ED's life became one big compromise: she did not retire from the world, like a cloistered nun, nor did she repress ego-transcendence. She became, as she says deprecatingly, "a Dedicated sort" (line 7).

She was dedicated to her vocation as witness/poet,

Yet not too far to come at call -
And do the little Toils
That make the Circuit of the Rest –

That is to say, "I am not so dedicated to my vocation that I cannot meet my everyday responsibilities that make up the Circuit of the Rest – the daily life of the other people I live with."

I am fond of quoting the Zen saying, "Before enlightenment, chopping wood & carrying water; after enlightenment, chopping wood & carrying water." This saying applies to ED's lifelong compromise as expressed in the present poem, & also in P-1223 ("Who goes to dine"), where she refers to the activities of her daily life as "ignoble Services."

In the last lines of the present poem ED acknowledges her gratitude to family & friends with whom she shares her daily life – but then apostrophizes them, as if to say, "Thank you for asking me to share life with you – but don't you know Whose invitation For Whom I must decline?"

1581

The farthest Thunder that I heard
Was nearer than the Sky
And rumbles still, though torrid Noons
Have lain their missiles by –
The Lightning that preceded it
Struck no one but myself –
But I would not exchange the Bolt
For all the rest of Life –
Indebtedness to Oxygen
The Happy may repay,
But not the obligation
To Electricity –
It founds the Homes and decks the Days
And every clamor bright
Is but the gleam concomitant
Of that waylaying Light –
The Thought is quiet as a Flake –
A Crash without a Sound,
How Life's reverberation
Its Explanation found –

THE WAYLAYING LIGHT

Here ED describes ego-transcendence as a dramatic electric storm: it struck her like a bolt of lightning, & "no one but myself":

> But I would not exchange the Bolt
> For all the rest of Life –

This was a solitary experience ("Struck no one but myself") which situated her among the "Happy [Few]" (line 10). These Happy Few are the same ones as the "imperial few" of P-1577 to whom ego-transcendence is vouchsafed. (Down through the ages they become the "ethereal throng" of P-1596). The transcendentalists are the Awakened Ones, who are able to "repay indebtedness to oxygen" (lines 9-10) by breathing, giving back what they have taken in. In essence the Breath of Life is ***spiritus*** (L. "air in motion"): when the ego-transcendent person breathes (as in breathing meditation) he or she takes in the spiritus & gives it back (the egocentric person simply expels stale air as one more form of waste matter).

On the other hand, the transcendentalist cannot repay the "obligation to electricity" (lines 11-12). Electricity in human form is libido, as in P-1431, where ego-transcendence is called an "electric gale," or in P-1585, where the creative act is called "electric Rest." Libido – the "animal magnetism" of Franz Mesmer (1734-1815) – is a given, life itself, by the grace of Mother Earth. It is the foundation of life on earth – but civilization is merely a "gleam concomitant / Of that waylaying Light" (lines 15-16). Human society coexists with the real power of consciousness, which is the power to "waylay" the human mind.

"Waylay" is especially trenchant here, because of its two meanings: (1) "to intercept or attack from ambush, as in order to rob, seize, or slay"; & (2) "to await and accost unexpectedly" (Random House Dictionary). Ego-transcendence is always unexpected, of course, a fact that never ceases to amaze the transcendentalist; in this respect it is like love at first sight. At the same time, ego-transcendence "attacks" & slays the ego-illusion. Compared to this sudden bolt of lightning, all the light of the egocentric consciousness is but a "gleam concomitant" (line 15).

What is especially striking is the fact that ego-transcendence is an entirely silent, inner event, "A Crash without a Sound" (line 18). It is the same Crash as that described in P-1503: "The Crash of nothing, yet of all," the crash of the ego-illusion (nothing), & the crash of all – the entire reality of maya, the everyday world in which ego has invested all its beliefs.[41]

ED calls ego-transcendence the "explanation of Life's reverberation." "Reverberate" means "to be reflected many times, as sound waves from the walls of a confined space." This is the beating heart itself, a muscle that mysteriously reverberates within the rib cage, many times a minute, year after year. Sudden enlightenment seems to account for the mystery: Mother Nature, in the form of Psyche, is striving to become conscious of Herself. The beating heart, the steady flow of electricity throughout the millennia, culminates in this astounding awareness, housed within the body of a single biped. This electric current may produce a "concomitant gleam" in the form of human societies & civilizations, but the "explanation" for this dogged persistence

41 See our commentary on P-1503, "More than the Grave is closed to me" (pp. 163-4).

appears evident in the phenomenon of enlightenment. So it seemed to the Buddha, & so it seems to ED.

1176

We never know how high we are
Till we are asked to rise
And then if we are true to plan
Our statures touch the skies –

The Heroism we recite
Would be a normal thing
Did not ourselves the Cubits warp
For fear to be a King –

"TRUE TO PLAN"

We human beings are unique in our ability to transcend instinct & to become individual ego-identities; we are also unique in our inborn ability to transcend the ego-identity, to ***individuate,*** if we live our lives "true to plan" [line 3].

This innate ability to deepen contact with Psyche [Nature] & the creative unconscious appears as part of an evolutionary "Plan," whereby Nature may become conscious of Herself.[42] ED coined different expressions for this phenomenon; as a poet of genius she saw how it manifested itself in her own being.

"Maturity of Fate" [P-990] is one such coinage. Everyone has a lower fate & a Higher Fate. It was ED's lower fate to live as a spinster in nineteenth-century Amherst; it was her Higher Fate to become ED. In P-990 she recalls that the awakening happened in a flash – "overnight" as it were:

> Maturity of Fate
> Is consummated equally
> In Ages, or a Night –

In P-856 ED calls Buddha Mind "the Eternal Function," as good a term as Jung's "Individuation Process." It is the universal function of consciousness in process of becoming transcendent Mind. Similarly, in P-290 ED says that her sense of non-ego reality is "preconcerted with itself." If you are born as a human being,

42 Many people are tempted to see evolutionary development as the unfolding of a Divine Plan, akin to the so-called Argument from Design..

then the stage is already set for actualizing Buddha Mind. As the Buddha himself said, we are all Buddhas already, whether or not we know this.

In P-803 our natural capacity to individuate is called simply one's "Own." This is the Self against which the ego is continually conspiring.

In P-822, our ability to individuate is called "the most profound experiment [experience] / appointed unto Men." "Appointed" is the operative work here, synonymous with "preconcerted."

In the present poem ED speaks of ego-transcendence as "rising to the skies."

We can all rise above the ego-level,

> And then if we are true to plan
> Our statures touch the skies –

In the second stanza ED goes on to say that what the world calls heroism could be normal,

> Did not ourselves the Cubits warp
> For fear to be a King –

This is one of ED's typically compressed coinages. "Cubit," as a linear measure from elbow to fingertip, is an archetypal dimension. She uses it elsewhere,[43] & I think that she likes it for two reasons: (1) it has strong biblical (archetypal) connotations, & (2) it refers specifically to the human body – the reach of the arm. As ordinary, everyday citizens, we "warp" our reach, turn it from its natural, "preconcerted" direction, shrink it, & ignore the fact of our human potential. We do this "For fear to be a King." "King" (like "Majesty," "Sire," "Sovereign," etc.) means Buddha

---

43 See poems 240, 405, 949, & 1178

Mind. This entails loss of our precious ego-values, & so fear of loss keeps us in our limited, provincial place.

232

The *Sun* – *just touched* the Morning –
The *Morning* – Happy thing –
Supposed that He had come to *dwell* –
And Life would all be *Spring*!

She felt herself *supremer* –
A *Raised* – *Ethereal Thing*!
Henceforth – for Her – *What Holiday*!
Meanwhile – Her wheeling King –
Trailed – slow – along the Orchards –
His *haughty* – *spangled* Hems –
Leaving a *new necessity*!
The *want* of *Diadems*!

The Morning – *fluttered* – *staggered* –
Felt feebly – for Her *Crown* –
Her *unanointed forehead* –
Henceforth – Her *only* One!

THE UNANOINTED BLISS

As a young woman Emily Dickinson began to experience episodes of ego-transcendence that astonished her. The Truth is always astonishing, of course, but also astonishing is the fact that it has happened to you, of all people. As a conventional ego-identity, "you" have suddenly experienced You, the Higher Self, Buddha Mind; from now on life is going to be wonderful. But then, unforeseen problems arise; life is not Simple, not One, after all: life has suddenly gotten very complicated.

In the present poem ED sees dawn breaking over town & finds in this a perfect metaphor for her own early naiveté regarding enlightenment. In her own ecstatic happiness she did not reckon with the Dark Night of the Soul, nor with the endless difficulties this momentous event would begin to create in her everyday life among family & friends. Her new-found mysticism, her Newfoundland, would certainly cause consternation. If she were to "come out" to family & friends, she would alienate them, like a gay coming out in society. It would set her apart as – what? An eccentric? A kook? Hysterical? Self-obsessed? Nuts? Her mysticism quickly turned into an existential problem, a predicament.

At the same time she knew that she had a vocation as a kind of nature poet, & that this bent was wholly in keeping with ego-transcendence, the return to Eden. This was life before the Fall, before the birth of ego. She had discovered ***maha–atman***, Great Self, just as Gandhi would do, & just as the Buddha had already done.

Her answer to the problem was to keep the Emily Dickinson

identity in place, & to be loyal to it, because it deserved her loyalty. At the same time, her vocation as witness/poet became clear: she would create poems celebrating the fact of ego-transcendence – sutras if you will – & she would compile them in the form of homemade booklets, to be treasured in secret:

> Deprived of other Banquet,
> I entertained Myself –
> At first – a scant nutrition –
> An insufficient Loaf –
>
> But grown by slender addings
> To so esteemed a size
> 'Tis sumptuous enough for me –
> And almost to suffice
>
> *(773)*

"Almost" is a bittersweet confession.

In the present poem ED sees the dawning as a metaphor for what has happened to her own consciousness. The Morning was the naïve ED herself, made possible by the rising sun, & she immediately congratulated herself:

> Supposed that He had come to *dwell* –
> And Life would all be *Spring*!
>
> She felt herself *supremer* –
> A *Raised Ethereal Thing*!
> Henceforth – for Her – *What Holiday*!

Meanwhile, Buddha Mind, her "wheeling King," rolled on beyond, & to her chagrin she suddenly felt "a ***new necessity***! [neediness]". She had no crown after all: her forehead was "unanointed." She would have to understand that her vocation as witness/poet was, as she says in P-365, her blacksmith poem, "an unanointed Blaze." "To anoint" means to confer official approval. Ego-transcendence needs no anointing. As the Zen adage puts it, "If you don't get it from yourself, where will you go for it?" ED ends the present poem by recognizing this transcendent fact of life. Transcendent consciousness is the "*only* One!" &, by definition must be unanointed.

356

The Day that I was crowned
Was like the other Days –
Until the Coronation came –
And then – 'twas Otherwise –

As Carbon in the Coal
And Carbon in the Gem
Are One – and yet the former
Were dull for Diadem –

I rose, and all was plain –
But when the Day declined
Myself and It, in Majesty
Were equally – adorned –

The Grace that I – was chose –
To Me – surpassed the Crown
That was the Witness for the Grace –
'Twas even that 'twas Mine –

I ROSE, AND ALL WAS PLAIN

This poem is typical of ED's descriptions of ego-transcendence, with its references to royalty, gems, & elevation from profane to sacred (here, coal to diamond).[44]

Enlightenment, as satori, is "sudden," meaning that it comes as a bolt out of the blue, with no preamble. In Zen Buddhism it often happens as the "answer" to a koan. Buddha Mind is experienced as the Great King of Reality, the ***maha–atman***. Thus,

The Day that I was crowned
Was like the other Days –
Until the Coronation came –
And then – 'twas Otherwise –

Stanza two concerns carbon in impure & pure forms (coal, diamond). "Carbon" is a metaphor for the Buddhanature inhering in every human soul. As a matter of fact, carbon, like the Buddhanature, is the basis of *all* organic matter, in impure form. In the diamond it is pure, like enlightened Buddha consciousness.

Line 9 describes ego-transcendence in six one-syllable words: "I rose, and all was plain." To "rise" in this way is a form of spiritual levitation; ED becomes One with Reality:

But when the Day declined
Myself and It, in Majesty
Were equally – adorned –

---

44 For Crown, see poems 608, 803, 1072, 1737, & 270 ("diadem"). See also the "***Gem***-tactics" of P-320.

The last stanza makes the point that the *Grace* of satori surpasses satori, just as the Grace of possessing genius may seem a greater gift than the genius itself. In nineteenth-century Amherst a young woman became enlightened, in a society that knew nothing about "enlightenment," & cared less: you've got Amherst, & you've got church – what more do you need? Nevertheless, one incredible day Emily Dickinson "rose, and all was plain." She was deeply humbled by this Grace.[45]

This phenomenon made ED "the witness for the Grace," hers to do with as she chose ("'twas Mine"). And so she became the poet/witness creating a new kind of sutra. Amherst eventually became known as the place where Emily Dickinson was born; it also happens to be the place where ED was born.

45 Claudio Arrau, the memorable Chilean pianist, was himself a transcendentalist, & always felt humbled by the strange fact that he, of all people (a poor Chilean yokel), should have been "chosen" to possess one of the great pianistic geniuses of the century.

1503

More than the Grave is closed to me –
The Grave and that Eternity
To which the Grave adheres –
I cling to nowhere till I fall –
The Crash of nothing, yet of all –
How similar appears –

THE CRASH OF NOTHING, YET OF ALL

All things swept sole away
This – is immensity –

(P-1512)

How much can come
And much can go,
And yet abide the World!

(From P-1593)

ED had a genius for naming spiritual events within, like a Buddhist scholar. Many of her poems are just that: creating a name for a spiritual event. P-1503 is such a poem.

She names ego-transcendence as "the Crash of Nothing, Yet of All." Ego-transcendence is a sudden awakening, a sudden destruction of the ego-identity. The ego-identity is suddenly seen to be an obvious illusion, a "nothing". So enlightenment is the Crash of Nothing. It's not as if "something" crashed, because ego never was a something.

At the same time Awakening is The Crash of All. This means everything in the phenomenal world of maya – everything that ego considers real. With Awakening "you" find "yourself" in the Full Void. Consciousness is empty of ego-identity; consciousness is ***anatman,*** not-self. This Void is suddenly flooded with Reality; its cup runneth over.

The Buddha's basic admonition is "Nothing whatsoever should be clung to as 'I' or 'mine'." Speaking with her own buddha voice ED says here, "I cling to nothing till I fall."

Enlightenment appears to be a foretaste of one's actual "fall" – death.

1555

I groped for him before I knew
With solemn nameless need
All other bounty sudden chaff
For this foreshadowed Food
Which others taste and spurn and sneer –
Though I within suppose
That consecrated it could be
The only Food that grows

GROPING

Dickinson's commentators like to speculate about her love life, & they keep an eye out for telltale signs in her poetry. One thinks of P-249, the famous "Wild Nights – Wild Nights!" In our discussion of P-1053 ("it was a quiet way") we point out the well-known similarity between transcendentalist discourse & profane love poetry; P-1053 begins

> It was a quiet way –
> He asked if I was his –
> I made no answer of the Tongue
> But answer of the Eyes –

This could be from a popular love ballad. If the writer is known to be a mystic (e.g., Rumi, St. John of the Cross), then there is no confusion. But if the poet is not recognized as a genuine mystic, then she gets a profane reading, even if it seems beyond common sense. P-276, "Many a phrase has the English language," concerns onomatopoeia as representing the sounds of Nature, which stir in ED a "push of Joy." Prof. Wolff, in ***Emily Dickinson***, sees this as an X-rated expression, & takes it to be the graphic description of a man copulating with the Belle of Amherst (p.368). This strikes me as quite funny, apart from the fact that there is nothing in the context of that detailed, 16-line poem to warrant seeing a sudden outburst of sexual excitement[46].

---

46 In P-252 ("I can wade Grief") ED uses the same expression: "... the least push of Joy / Breaks up my feet – / And I tip—drunken..."

The above remarks are by way of discussing P-1555, which begins

> I groped for him before I knew
> With solemn nameless need

A profane reading of these lines would have ED sexually fondling an unnamed lover. There is nothing to prevent this reading, unless you can establish it as anachronistic (difficult to do). But it seems highly unlikely that ED is being sexually graphic here. It reads like transcendentalist love poetry, where "groping" means "seeking blindly": one intuits an ego-transcendent presence in the heart, & senses that it can be raised to consciousness (see "foreshadowed" in line 4).

The poem goes on to develop the theme of heavenly food, common enough in ED's poetry (along with heavenly riches), as in P-1223:

> Who goes to dine must take his Feast
> Or find the Banquet mean –
> The Table is not laid without
> Till it is laid within.

(The interested reader may consult poems 612, 690, 773, 1240, 1262, 1282, & 1377).

Lines 4-5 of the present poem read:

> For this foreshadowed Food
> Which others taste and spurn and sneer –

This is a common transcendentalist criticism of egocentrism, & evokes ch.41 of the ***Tao Te Ching,*** quoted previously (see p.125).

When a wise scholar hears the Tao,
He practices it diligently.
When a mediocre scholar hears the Tao,
He wavers between belief and unbelief.
When a worthless scholar hears the Tao,
He laughs boisterously at it.

In the last two lines ED declares of this spiritual Food,

That consecrated it could be
The only Food that grows

I punctuate them this way: "[I suppose] that, consecrated, it could be / The only Food that grows." If ego-transcendence as ED knows it could be formally recognized, it could be the only spiritual sustenance required. Theistic churchgoers are notoriously unsustained by the Sunday rituals & sermons of the ordained middlemen. ED, storing her sutras away, had little idea that she was expressing the Buddhists' point of view: the real spiritual food must come from within. Blind faith in a theology is on the side of ego & its need for an afterlife.

1436

Than Heaven more remote
For Heaven is the root,
But these the flitted seed,
More flown indeed
Than ones that never were,
Or those that hide, and are.

What madness, by their side,
A vision to provide
Of future days
They cannot praise.

My soul, to find them, come,
They cannot call, they're dumb,
Nor prove, nor woo,
But that they have abode
Is absolute as God,
And instant, too.

THE FLITTED SEED

ED uses "Heaven" in two ways, (1) to denote the Christian idea of the afterlife, & (2) as a synonym for ecstasy, bliss, rapture, transport, & the like.[47] Ego-transcendence reveals the dharma, the empty nature of reality uninhabited by the ego-self – the "unfurnished Rooms" of P-393, & the "unfurnished eyes" of P-685.

"Dharma" is derived from the Sanskrit root ***dhr***, "to bear or support."[48] It is blissfully experienced as the Ground of Reality, hence "Heaven is the root" (line 2), as in P-1234:

> Mortality's Ground Floor
> Is Immortality –

ED's immediate subject here is the "flitted seed." By "flit" ED means "fly away into the air."[49] A flitted seed is one of the many scattered by plants exposed to seasonal winds. These seeds are contrasted with those that "hide" (line 6). The flitted seeds are more remote than the Christian Heaven, because "Heaven" is actually the experience of the Root of Reality, the dharma. The Christian Heaven is "remote" (far up above), but the dharma is far more remote to the ego-self. Once you experience Buddha Mind you realize just how remote it is from ego. The flitted seed

---

47 See poems 172, 1012, 1205, 1408, & 1544.

48 Damien Keown, ***A Dictionary of Buddhism.***

49 The interested reader may study ED's use of "flit" in poems 291, 572, 673, 854, 1257, 1455, 1509, & 1533.

occupies a place in reality between the seed that never made it, & the seed that hides, & is (line 6).

Now this poem begins to sound more & more like a description of ED herself (cf. P-1255, "Longing is like the Seed"). As poet/witness she is living her life somewhere between the seed that never makes it, & the seed that "hides, & is," the seed that becomes a plant, but is never liberated from its static existence in place & time.

Lines 7-10 describe the "madness" that ED adopted as her way of life:

> A vision to provide
> Of future days
> They cannot praise.

These seeds (ED uses "seed" as a collective noun) are scattered to the winds, & fall elsewhere at random (I take "by their side" to mean "on their part"). Such was to be the fate of ED's poetry, stashed away, only to find an accidental, posthumous fate. We, now of what to her were "future days," find the canon to be a special vision provided by the seed of her inspiration. ED appeared to leave it all to chance. What madness!

Being poet/witness was ED's karma, not a means to anything else. Indeed, her way of living has much in common with Joseph Cornell (1903-72), the great box artist, who spent most of his creative life in obscurity, immersed in the samadhi play of his vision. When he was eventually "discovered," he stubbornly resisted attempts to market his boxes. As he saw it, they were not merchandise, they were his children, & he was responsible for their welfare. Cynical art dealers thought him "mad" for being indifferent to the marketplace.

Both ED & Cornell were engrossed in their samadhi play,

providing a vision "Of future days / They cannot praise" (lines 9-10).

In the last stanza ED expresses an empathy with the flitted seed, for she is "by their side":

> My soul, to find them, come,
> They cannot call, they're dumb,
> Nor prove, nor woo,
> But that they have abode
> Is absolute as God,
> And instant, too.

ED's soul – her poetic voice – comes to give voice to the dharma – the flitted seed, in this case. They do not "prove" anything, nor do they woo (as does the published poet); but ED's poetic voice comes to find the spirit of the dharma, where everything is interconnected, & has an "abode" (line 14). The dharma "Is absolute as God" (line 15) – "And instant, too." It is ***Now***. The dharma, as non-ego reality, is not relative to anything else.

1410

I shall not murmur if at last
The ones I loved below
Permission have to understand
For what I shunned them so –
Divulging it would rest my Heart
But it would ravage theirs –
Why, Katie, Treason has a Voice –
But mine – dispels – in Tears.

TAKING REFUGE IN BUDDHA MIND

This poem, from the late 1870s, concerns ED's life as a recluse, but it should not be read too literally, as an egocentric social problem, so to speak. One biographer, Alfred Habegger, calls this poem at "tearful excuse" for ED's refusal to see an old friend, Catharine Scott Anthon.[50]

While ED certainly came to "shun" people, it is also true that more & more she came to "shun" Emily Dickinson, the ego-self. This is typically true of the transcendentalist.[51] P-642, "Me from Myself – to banish," the "mutual Monarch" poem, is a basic statement concerning this inner struggle; it is a veritable civil war, as we have noted in our earlier discussion of P-594:

> The Battle fought between the Soul
> And No Man – is the One
> Of all the Battles prevalent –
> By far the Greater One –

Conventional egocentric people have little idea that such a struggle is even possible. In the present poem ED says she will not "murmur" (complain) if her loved ones "Permission have to understand" for ***what*** she "shunned them so." This ***what*** is the issue, & does not mean an "excuse" (tearful or not); it means the ***reason***. Egocentric people would be baffled by ED's avoidance

50 *My Wars Are Laid Away In Books,* 536.

51 In our own time, Ram Dass is the best-known example: after his pilgrimage to India, he came to "shun" the ego-self known as Richard Alpert.

of them, & would likely take it personally. They would have to have "Permission" to understand it, authorization, as it were. In other words, they themselves would have to be vouchsafed an Awakening, an experience of the Higher Self.

By the late 1870s, ED had spent 40+ years stashing away her transcendentalist poems; if she were simply to "divulge" her secret now, it would "ravage" the hearts of her family & friends, because they would not be in any position to grasp her meaning. They would likely mourn her loss of sanity.

Pema Chodron, a veteran Buddhist nun & author well known in Buddhist circles, describes the "civil war" that usually occurs after the experience of ego-transcendence:

> You don't want to go back to the narrow perspective of this habitual mind [ego-self]. But you also realize that the narrow perspective gives you a lot of security. You know it's false security, a lie, but starting to wake up is a lot like giving up an addiction. You're going to go through withdrawal symptoms, weaning yourself from this addiction to habitual, small-minded patterns of perception. You could say enlightenment is no more addiction. You're just fully awake, fully on the spot, without having to hide out.[52]

ED, as she grew older, hid out less & less in the person of Emily Dickinson. But in the present poem, ED, apostrophizing Katie, assures her that she shouldn't take it personally. The "shunning" has nothing to do with "Treason," or betrayal. Treason is the voice of ego, & always has a reason for its negative actions; but ED's voice is not that of Emily Dickinson, & so cannot explain the matter to Emily Dickinson's circle of friends. The voice of ED can only "dispel" (die away) in tears – compassionate sorrow.

---

52 From an interview in *Tricycle* (Fall, 1993), 93.

1421

Such are the inlets of the mind –
His outlets – would you see
Ascend with me the eminence
Of immortality –

> Religious experience is that experience wherein the self, bursting through the screen of conditioning erected by thought and language, reunites with things as they are.[53]

EXPRESSION OF SELF, NOT "SELF-EXPRESSION"

The terse description above describes enlightenment in a nutshell. It appears in an article in ***Tricycle***, by Victor Sogen Hori, concerning the difference between American Buddhism & Asian Buddhism. Ego is the big difference, of course. Americans define themselves as autonomous, separate individuals; Asians much less so, for to them one's self & one's family are interwoven to a very high degree (hence the institutionalized "ancestor worship"). For the American, enlightenment means transcending the ego-self; for the Asian (as Hori explains) enlightenment means

> Breaking habits of selfishness in order to become open, responsible, and compassionate with others; meditation is personal reconditioning designed ultimately to dissolve attachment...[54]

Hence ***compassion*** is the core value of Buddhism, whereas Christianity focuses on the eternal salvation of the ego-self.

These considerations are relevant to the equation Emily Dickinson/ED, because Emily Dickinson was raised to be a member of her social class, with strong family ties; but her

53 Victor Sogen Hori, in ***Tricycle*** (Fall, '94), 52.

54 Ibid, 49.

transcendent experience led her, a Westerner, to focus on ***shedding*** an ego-identity interwoven with such ties. P-1410, just examined, approaches this theme of estrangement; the present poem is an epigram inviting one to follow her "outlet."

She says that the mind has inlets & outlets. In terms of everyday Western experience, the "inlet/outlet" dialectic refers to social conditioning (inlet, input), & "self-expression" (outlet). In this sense the epigram means "Social imprinting on the mind is "such" (so powerful) that if you want to experience a true outlet (transcendence), you'll have to come to the mountaintop with me." "Me" means Buddha Mind: when I study ED's sutras, I accompany her to the mountaintop.

The transcendental meaning of inlet/outlet comes from the idea of the mind as an inlet of the sea, "Ocean Mind." The inlet is "such" that if you want to see the "outlet" of the mind – its means of expression – come to the mountaintop with ED as your Sherpa.

1500

It came his turn to beg –
The begging for the life
Is different from another Alms
"Tis Penury in Chief –

I scanned his narrow realm
I gave him leave to live
Lest Gratitude revive the snake
Though smuggled his reprieve

PENURY IN CHIEF: THE NARROW REALM

Like P-446, "I showed her Heights she never saw," this poem contrasts the two basic "realms" of Psyche, ego & non-ego. These two realms are in a constant rivalry, so to speak, because of the proprietary jealousy with which the ego-identity tries to maintain its despotic hold over Psyche.

ED refers to the ego-identity as masculine, "It came his turn to beg," which is not unusual; in P-1499 she says

> How firm Eternity must look
> To crumbling men like me...

In the conventional personality the ego-identity takes itself for granted, like Descartes' ***ego*** (***cogito ergo sum***); here, it is non-ego that "goes begging." But with the joyful experience of ego-transcendence, it comes ego's turn to beg for its continued existence.

Begging for one's life is the most extreme for of begging – it is "Penury in Chief," by analogy with Commander in Chief.[55] ED, as Commander in Chief, is merciful, & gives ego "leave to live."

This ED poem, like many a Buddhist sutra, is a psychological analysis of what happens within Psyche when enlightenment occurs, & the full meaning of her text here must be understood in terms of "Gratitude" (line 7). She is referring to her gratitude for enlightenment. When this grace descends upon you, you

---

55 Spelled with or without hyphens. The term goes back centuries, & it figures prominently in the U.S. Constitution (Article II, Section 2).

feel a huge sense of thankfulness: I am so grateful for this grace bestowed upon *me*!

This point has always been a big issue among serious meditators. When one experiences satori, or realization, this may be deep or shallow, with regard to detachment from ego. Shallow realization easily becomes a matter for self-congratulation, as described by one American Zen practitioner in Kapleau's ***The Three Pillars of Zen***: having traveled to Japan in order to practice in a monastery, he wrote, "Won't my Zen friends in the United States be envious when I write I have satori!" (230) As Kapleau explains,

> Enlightenment, while revealing our solidarity with all things, …paradoxically gives rise to a fine mist of pride in such an accomplishment, and this mars the inherent purity of the Mind. (300)

Harada-roshi, one of the Zen masters quoted by Kapleau, writes,

> An ancient Zen saying has it that to become attached to one's own enlightenment is as much a sickness as to exhibit a maddeningly active ego. … Those who practice Zen must guard against [this]. My own sickness lasted almost ten years. Ha! (302)

Of course ED felt much gratitude for the experience of ego-transcendence, but she also recognized the danger (she had to be her own guru): this very gratitude could become a new, deadly form of ego, an asp in her bosom as it were. So she resolved to settle for the old, unassuming ego-identity, even though satori had shown it to be a mere illusion. She gave it a reprieve – "smuggled" in it, as if it were ontologically legal, even though it was not. As she says in P-1741,

Believing what we don't believe
Does not exhilarate.

The Emily Dickinson ego-identity may not exhilarate, but neither is it a holier-than-thou ego-persona. Her family & friends were none the wiser – nor were all the "puzzled scholars" who came later.

Before enlightenment, chopping wood & fetching water; after enlightenment, chopping wood & fetching water.

Zen proverb.

1502

I saw the wind within her
I knew it blew for me –
But she must buy my shelter
I asked Humility

TAKING REFUGE

This poem is partner to P-1500 as a further commentary on the difficult alliance between ego & non-ego, regarding the problem of living one's everyday life. ED says that she "saw the wind within her," the spiritus arising in the soul of Emily Dickinson, & that she "knew it blew for me." In P-1500 ED says of the ego-identity, "I gave him leave to live"; now she attaches a condition: "she must buy my shelter."

This could have two distinct meanings (& perhaps is intended to have them both): (1) Emily Dickinson must buy the shelter offered by ED, or (2) Emily Dickinson must buy the shelter needed by ED.

"To buy" means generally "to obtain, to acquire by exchange." If the Higher Self is to predominate in Psyche, then the ego-identity must cede its normally dominant position in exchange for the spiritual refuge offered by the Great Self (just as the Buddhists regularly declare, "I take shelter in the Buddha").

At the same time, "buying my shelter" may well mean arranging daily life so as to accommodate or shelter the continuing Presence of the Higher Self.

The Buddhists recognize the two general phases of enlightenment: (1) realization, & (2) actualization. Realization is satori; actualization means integrating enlightenment into one's everyday life, i.e. learning how to give it permanent shelter.

The last line says, "I asked Humility," which reflects the thought of P-1500, in reference to the need for continued detachment from ego, & its pride in a spiritual "accomplishment." ED must find the humility to continue living her life as an ordinary Emily Dickinson, just as the Zen saying has it: "Before enlightenment..."

1442

To mend each tattered Faith
There is a needle fair
Though no appearance indicate –
"Tis threaded in the Air –

And though it do not wear
As if it never Tore
"Tis very comfortable indeed
And spacious as before –

BACK HOME AGAIN: THE RENOVATIO

Ego-transcendence teaches a new meaning of the word "faith." Theistic religions require "blind faith," belief not based on proof; ego-transcendence, on the other hand, is a floodlight of awareness, & creates a ***faith*** in the sense of confidence & trust, just as one has faith in a close friend's integrity because it has been earned over the years.

ED's own religious faith had become tattered & torn, as she says in the present poem, but her awakening to Buddha Mind renovated her sense of faith in a higher truth. As she says in P-172,

> For Heaven is a different thing,
> Conjectured, and waked sudden in –

Her awakening had mended her faith, as a garment might be made like new by an expert seamstress. This is accomplished with the aid of a "needle fair," "threaded in the Air" – the pervasive Spiritus of the dharma. The experience of ego-transcendence generates a ***renovatio*** [to use the traditional term], a renewal of reality, whole once again, "As if it never Tore." It is comfortable "And spacious as before" – before the dual thinking of "socialization" separated the self from the dharma.

963

A nearness to Tremendousness –
An Agony procures –
Affliction ranges Boundlessness –
Vicinity to Laws

Contentment's quiet Suburb –
Affliction cannot stay
In Acres – Its Location
Is Illocality –

DON'T FENCE ME IN

"Tremendous(ness)" refers to the enhanced consciousness of ego-transcendence, just as "stupendous(ness)" in P-1309:

> The Infinite a sudden Guest
> Has been assumed to be –
> But how can that stupendous come
> Which never went away?

in P-802 ego-transcendence is a "Stupendous Vision."

ED is talking about being on the threshold of ego-transcendence, the "nearness to Tremendousness." This is where the "Agony" takes place. "Agony" is used in the sense of "death struggle," the ***transitus*** entailing ego-death ("turning on"); this becomes nirvana (Skt, "extinction"). ED says that the nearness (threshold) "procures" this Agony. "Procure" is used here in the Latin sense of "to manage, to see to" (as in "procurator").[56]

This "afflicts" the ego-self as it "ranges Boundlessness," as it explores the open range of unconditioned mind. Egocentric contentment dwells in a "quiet Suburb," but the affliction of ego-transcendence "cannot stay / In Acres," i.e., measurable boundaries that the good citizens all agree upon ("Vicinity to Laws"). The "location" of ego-transcendence is no location at all; it is "Illocality." "Illocality" is a coinage that echoes "illogical," & it means "without a locus, or place." It also recalls "utopia" ("bliss"), meaning "not a place." Ego-transcendence has no locus, just as utopia has no topography.

---

56 This meaning is retained on modern Sp. ***procurar***, & Ital. ***procurare***.

The entire poem is a sophisticated, or “cool” description of what it’s like to pass over from ego-mind to non-ego mind.

1195

What we see we know somewhat
Be it but a little –
What we don't surmise we do
Though it shows so fickle

I shall vote for Lands with Locks
Granted I can pick 'em –
Transport's doubtful Dividend
Patented by Adam.

1354

The Heart is the Capital of the Mind –
The Mind is a single State –
The Heart and the Mind together make
A single Continent –

One – is the Population –
Numerous enough –
This ecstatic Nation
Seek – it is Yourself.

"My brain is the key that sets me free"

–Harry Houdini, "America's Self-Liberator" [57]

A DIVIDEND OF ENLIGHTENMENT

Using the royal we, ED contrasts the uncertain, limited knowledge of the little self with the certain knowledge of the awakened mind, when we do indeed know. Episodes of transcendence are "fickle" (line 4), because they are unpredictable.

ED likened Psyche to the idea of nation, land, state, or country, as in P-1354, quoted above, or in P-905:

Between My Country – and the Others –
There is a Sea –

"Land," as a metaphor for the socialized ego-identity (i.e., one is a New Englander, a Texan, etc.) is, for most people, a sealed-in space, like a prison in which they spend their entire lives. They are "locked in," or "landlocked" (a pun implied here by ED), never suspecting that it is possible to venture beyond its limits. The "natural-born" transcendentalist, however, grows up taking it for granted that he or she can "pick the lock" & escape to regions unknown, as ED says in an early poem (P-77):

I never hear the word "escape"
Without a quicker blood,

---

57 Houdini wrote this motto as part of his autograph. See ***Art & Antiques*** (May, 2005), 34. ED was clearly aware of the phenomenon.

A sudden expectation,
A flying attitude!

Enlightenment is the highest experience possible for a human being, of course; at the same time there is a bonus, or dividend, as it were: the Awakened One realizes & appreciates the ego-identity because it is this which enables ego-transcendence to occur! Without ego the thrill of ego-transcendence is impossible. So ED "votes for" Lands with locks, because she can "pick 'em." She is a transcendentalist Houdini.

Every lock implies the existence of a key, & ego implies the existence of non-ego. There have always existed countless ego-identities, all arising from a common tabula rasa. This idea appears in a poem by Chiyo-ni, the best-known woman haiku writer:

A hundred different gourds
From the mind
Of one vine.

(Blyth, 1102)

Everyone who transcends ego awakens to the same Buddha mind.

The last two lines of the present poem refer to

Transport's doubtful Dividend
Patented by Adam.

"Transport" is the episode of ego-transcendence, or course, as ED likes to call it.[58] The transport here is a "doubtful Dividend / Patented by Adam."

58 See, for example, poems 137, 157, 166, 184, 481, 984, 1109, 1279, 1413.

The Eden myth is the Christian version of the birth of ego-consciousness. With the birth of ego (the ability to discriminate) the bliss of unconditioned awareness disappears. The thrill of ego-transcendence depends upon the prior existence of ego, which now functions as a dividend, or bonus. If it is "doubtful," this is because the fickle appearance & non-appearance of enlightenment generates the Dark Night of the Soul.

1656

Down Time's quaint stream
Without an oar
We are enforced to sail
Our Port a secret
Our Perchance a Gale
What Skipper would
Incur the Risk
What Buccaneer would ride
Without a surety from the Wind
Or schedule of the Tide –

THE QUAINT CALENDAR

> Quaint. Having an old-fashioned charm. Peculiar or unusual in an interesting or amusing way.
>
> Random House Dictionary

The key word in this poem is "quaint," which ED uses to describe the flow of time: "Time's quaint stream." A person who finds something to be quaint is one who has gone far beyond the viewpoint or perspective expressed by the "quaint" thing: a "quaint village," a "quaint attitude." Certainly the term implies condescension.

Clock time seems unreal – or quaint, or absurd – to the transcendentalist who has experienced life beyond clock time, as described in P-287, "A Clock stopped." Life is a ceaseless Becoming in the Eternal Now. Clock time suddenly becomes passé, so to speak, just as ego itself seems passé – nay, quaint. "I [ego] think, therefore I am" is indeed a quaint philosophy. For ego, clock time is part of the world "out there," where Time Marches On, & eventually crushes ego.[59] But in the Eternal Now there is no such separateness. One's consciousness *is* the Eternal Now, & the Eternal Now *is* who one is. This is what the Hindus call sat-chit-ananda, being-consciousness-bliss.

So ego, condemned by the calendar & the clock, is up the

---

59 Many – perhaps most – modern birthday cards convey this attitude, though in a joking way: for the adult, each new birthday is a misfortune, & aging is a bummer.

creek without a paddle – or down the stream without an oar, as ED says (lines 1-2).

In line 3, ED says, "We are enforced…" I take this to be ED's use of the royal we, rather than a general reference to everybody. Understanding many of her poems depends crucially upon how we understand "we." In the present poem ED is referring to her own experience as a transcendentalist in situ, as it were. Some transcendentalists retire from the world, & become recluses, or cloistered loners; but ED has determined to live her life in the midst of family & friends. Hence she finds herself "enforced" to sail on their quaint stream. Her Port, or guiding star, must be kept secret, just as her growing stash of poems, as she says in P-1737:

> Big my Secret but it's *bandaged* –
> It will never get away

Her "Perchance," or lot, in life includes Gales, as she knows. Ego-transcendence may be experienced as a violent storm, as she says in P-1745: "a hurricane / In a congenial ground."[60] Experienced skippers – & buccaneers – depend upon their maritime knowledge to determine conditions for setting sail; but for the transcendentalist sailor there is no such knowledge available. The Gales, the Winds, the Tides of spiritual fortune transcend all possible ego-knowledge, & cannot be related to any previous experience such as that recounted in bibles & holy texts. These are all hearsay.

Thus ED, as an existential sailor, is completely on her own, & must incur the Risk of braving the spiritual storms that beset her. In the early poem P-172, she saw this "Risk" as a great existential gamble:

---

60 Regarding this kind of spiritual storm, see especially ED poems 315, 362, 974, & 1581.

'Tis so much joy! 'Tis so much joy!
If I should fail, what poverty!
And yet, as poor as I,
Have ventured all upon a throw!

The present poem is a late one, & mellow at that: she can gaze upon the egocentric world surrounding her, & regard it as "quaint" – no longer a threat.

1604

We send the Wave to find the Wave –
An Errand so divine,
The Messenger enamored too,
Forgetting to return,
We make the wise distinction still,
Soever made in vain,
The sagest time to dam the sea is when the sea is gone –

REMEMBERING TO RETURN

> Our minds are just waves on the ocean of consciousness. As waves they come and go. As ocean they are infinite and eternal. Know yourself as the ocean of being, the womb of all existence.[61]

In the present poem ED states that when we open the Heart/Mind to non-ego awareness, "We send the Wave to find the Wave," to experience oneself as integral to the ocean tides. Ego-transcendence may result in a bliss so great that one forgets to return (line 4). This observation lies at the heart of what the Buddhists call the ***bodhisattva***, the Enlightened One who postpones entering nirvana until all sentient beings are saved; that is to say, the bodhisattva ***remembers to return***. ED's way of remembering to return was to become the poet/witness, addressing all of us sentient beings who read her poetry.

This poem ends with an epigram: "The sagest time to dam the sea is when the sea is gone." The everyday ego-identity represents the time "when the sea is gone." This is the best time to "dam the sea," protect the ego-identity from its frequent annihilation. ED is aware of this distinction, but it is "soever" ("in any case") "made in vain."

The "we" of this poem clearly seems to be the royal we, ED herself. Here it is relevant to quote the first stanza of P-160, where, using the first person singular, she describes a "near miss":

---

61 Nisargadatta Maharaj, *I Am That*, 253.

Just lost, when I was saved!
Just felt the world go by!
Just girt me for the onset with Eternity,
When breath blew back,
And on the other side
I heard recede the disappointed tide!

Sometimes ego-transcendence "almost" occurs, but then – like a failed orgasm – the aura dies down & the "disappointed tide" is gone.

284

The Drop, that wrestles in the Sea –
Forgets her own locality –
As I – toward Thee –

She know herself as an incense small –
Yet *small* – she sighs – if *All* – is *All* –
How *larger* – be?

The Ocean – smiles – at her Conceit –
But *she*, forgetting Amphitrite –
Pleads – "Me"?

OCEANIC CONSCIOUSNESS

In Buddhist teaching the wave/ocean connection is a traditional image for the relationship between the individual mind & oceanic, unconditioned awareness. The Dalai Lama's title, in fact, means "Oceanic Lama." Buddhist Master Thich Nhat Hanh explains the wave/ocean connection in this way:

> A wave is a wave, but at the same time it is water. The wave does not have to die in order to become water; it is already water right in the present moment. ... To talk about a wave we need these notions: the wave arises and passes away; ...it has a beginning and an end... But none of these distinctions can be applied to the wave in its ultimate dimension as water. In fact, you cannot separate the wave from its ultimate dimension.

Nhat goes on to point out that Buddhist practice:

> Is to become like a wave – while living the life of a wave in the historical dimension, we realize that we are also water and live the life of water. That is the essence of the practice.[62]

The wave/ocean connection is a natural one that occurs whenever people experience "oceanic consciousness" (hence the term). One is not "drifting" on this ocean, one is absorbed by it, all the while mindful of it. One is profoundly grateful for the

---

62 These quotes are from ***Buddhadharma***, (Spring, 2004), pp. 19-20.

experience, & one thanks Buddha Mind, whom ED addresses here as "Thee." Her daily ego-identity is the "locality" she forgets. Ego is indeed a "wrestling" drop of water, struggling to maintain belief in itself as a discrete drop of water (as if there could ever be such a thing in Waterworld).

She voices the obvious paradox: if ego-consciousness seems "small," it is still part of the All – so how can the ocean be larger than the wave? Buddha Mind – the Ocean – smiles at her conceit (metaphor) – accepts it as part of who ED is; but ED still "Pleads – 'Me'?" She "pleads" this, "forgetting Amphitrite."

Amphitrite (which ED cagily rhymes with "conceit") was the daughter of Nereus & the consort of Poseidon, all ancient Greek divinities of the Ocean. ED here recognizes their function as gods of a polytheistic religion. A major value of polytheistic religions is how they allow each believer to identify with the god most compatible with his or her own temperament, much like the Roman Catholic calendar of saints. Amphitrite was an individual divine woman – & at the same time part of who Nereus & Poseidon were. In the present poem ED is saying that she is "forgetting" – meaning remembering – that ego-transcendence turns her into a "divine woman." There is no need to plead for her identity as ED.

1462

We knew not that we were to live –
Nor when – we are to die –
Our ignorance – our cuirass is –
We wear Mortality
As lightly as an Option Gown
Till asked to take it off –
By his intrusion, God is known –
It is the same with Life –

MAN'S EXTREMITY IS GOD'S OPPORTUNITY

While ignorance may not be "bliss," it can protect us from obsessing about future calamity. Buddhists sometimes say that we are all living on death row, & while it is a striking analogy, it isn't accurate, because no date has been set for our "execution" (so far as we know). In the present poem ED makes this point. Our ignorance is like a cuirass (body armor) allowing us to live as carefree as we like. She says that we wear our mortality

> As lightly as an Option Gown
> Till asked to take it off –

I've not found the expression "option gown" elsewhere, but it is very close to our modern use of "optional" in reference to dress. For "optional" the Random House Dictionary gives, for example, "Formal dress is optional [1755-65]."

In the last two lines of this poem ED gives a transcendentalist twist to an otherwise conventional idea:

> By his intrusion, God is known –
> It is the same with Life –

Anyone's death may be regarded as an "intrusion of God" (cf. "act of God"), when God makes his presence known; but ED goes on to say, "It is the same with Life." The occurrence of ego-death (satori) is also an intrusion of "God" in the form of the Higher Self, or Buddha Mind. It intrudes upon the expected continuity of our life in clock time; for ED, it changed entirely the existential terms of her life on earth.

4. LIBERATION MAY BE ATTAINED THROUGH MEDITATION & RIGHT CONDUCT

THE NOBLE EIGHTFOLD PATH

The Fourth Noble Truth concerns the Eightfold Path as the means of ending suffering with the attainment of nirvana (extinction of ego-self):

1. right understanding
2. right thought
3. right speech
4. right action
5. right livelihood
6. right effort
7. right mindfulness
8. right meditation

Commentators variously explain that "right" means "appropriate," "wise," "seeing versus not seeing," or "whole." I think of it as meaning "non-ego" – "non-ego understanding," non-ego thought," etc. This seems inevitable after ego-transcendence has been realized: how can you "un-initiate" yourself & return to the old egocentric ways?

Even if this were possible, it is clear from ED's oeuvre that once she found herself on the higher path, she recognized that she was fully committed to it. Her poetry quite naturally embodies the Eightfold Path in the form of non-ego understanding, thought, speech, action, effort, mindfulness, & meditation. Livelihood, the fifth part, is a special case, since she had no need to earn her livelihood; but she was a poet by calling, so she made it a non-ego labor of love.

Creating a transcendentalist poem involves a concentrated application of the Noble Eightfold Path. The process begins, of course, with right (non-ego) mindfulness & right (non-ego) meditation. The work itself obviously demands right understanding, right thought, and right speech, above all! Writing the poem down & making a fair copy is right action & right effort. So the Noble Eightfold Path may rightly be regarded as the Buddhist esthetic for the transcendentalist poet.

1262

I cannot see my soul but know 'tis there
Nor ever saw his house nor furniture,
Who has invited me with him to dwell;
But a confiding guest consult as well,
What raiment honor him the most,
That I be adequately dressed,
For he insures to none
Lest men specifical adorn
Procuring him perpetual drest
By dating it a sudden feast.

THE WHITE DRESS: REALIZING, ACTUALIZING

He was my host – he was my guest,
I never to this day
If I invited him could tell,
Or he invited me.

(From P-1721)

For ED an episode of ego-transcendence is experienced as a Visit, or Visitation. Several times she speaks of the Guest/Host relationship, where the Higher Self is sometimes Guest, sometimes Host.[63]

In the present poem the soul (line 1) embodies the Higher Self as the Host, who has honored her with His invitation, & for whom one dons ritual dress (the "raiment" of line 5). This is the famous white dress adopted by ED (evoking the right action of the Noble Eightfold Path). She discusses her garb in terms of what the Host may or may not "insure (line 7).

Insure/ensure are interchangeable, & I believe that "insure" here is meant in the sense of "guarantee." As transcendentalists know only too well, Buddha Mind makes no guarantee regarding its "invitations," or its "visitations." This is as if "He" were forestalling attempts to lure him with ritual & festive robes. In

63 See poems 446, 674, 817, 1055, 1060, 1309, & 1721. The two words "guest" & "host" are cognate & reciprocal, from L. ***hospes, -pitis***; the double meaning is preserved in modern Sp. ***huésped***. "Host," in the present sense, should not be confused with the "host" of the Roman Catholic mass (from L. ***hostia***, "victim").

the Roman Catholic mass this is what the officiant appears to be doing, dressed appropriately for any given feast day,

> Procuring him perpetual drest
> By dating it a sudden feast.

I read the last three lines of this poem as meaning, "Lest men specifically adorn themselves, regularly dressed in ritual attire, regarding the Visitation as an instant feast." It is as if the officiant were a procurator, bringing about the appearance of the Holy Ghost: he raises the chalice, a bell sounds – & lo! The Holy Ghost is conjured!

ED herself took to being "perpetual drest" in white, which is her tabula rasa, evoking the virgin mind of non-ego consciousness. In the long term, however, it is not festive raiment, or even ritual raiment; it is a way of avoiding the street clothes of the conventional citizens of Amherst.

As we have noted elsewhere, the Buddhists distinguish between "realization" & "actualization." Realization is satori, the sudden episode of ego-transcendence, evoking the Third Noble Truth regarding nirvana ("extinction"). Actualization is the incorporation of the Noble Eightfold Path into one's everyday ego-identity, which produces the serene presence typical of veteran gurus & roshis.

Hence the task of actualization concerns a disciplined lifestyle in the long term. The monastic orders were created for this purpose, & necessarily include a prescribed way of dressing, usually a simple robe in a given color. ED was intuitively drawn to a quasi-monastic life.

1277

While we were fearing it, it came –
But came with less of fear
Because that fearing it so long
Had almost made it fair –

There is a Fitting – a Dismay –
A Fitting – a Despair –
'Tis harder knowing it is Due
Than knowing it is Here.

The Trying on the Utmost
The Morning it is new
Is Terribler than wearing it
A whole existence through.

1181

When I hoped I feared –
Since I hoped I dared
Everywhere alone
As a Church remain –
Spectre cannot harm –
Serpent cannot charm –
He deposes Doom
Who hath suffered him –

1360

I sued the News – yet feared – the News
That such a Realm could be –
"The House not made with Hands" it was –
Thrown open wide to me –

THE FITTING: MORE ON THE WHITE DRESS

Poems 1181 & 1360 are included here with P-1277 in order to help understand & document the *fear* instilled by ego-loss. This may be especially severe when the person has no clear idea of what kind of transformation is taking place.

Anyone reared in a Buddhist or Hindu culture would probably not be so easily overwhelmed by ego-loss – & in any case would soon find a support system. In nineteenth-century America, any deep epiphany would take on the trappings of a theistic religion, as happened regularly at the tent revival meetings popular in ED's time.

But ED, with a strong individualistic genius for self-realization, was destined to write her own bible, her own sutras, free of any structure imposed from without. As she says in P-1360, this new world was "The House not made with Hands" – meaning not simply that it was spiritual, but also it was entirely original, "untouched by human hands."

In P-1277 ED is using the royal we, I believe, & she is tracing the spiritual path she has experienced to date, in the person of Emily Dickinson.[64] In the first stanza she implies that her spiritual awakening, as it gathered momentum, began to dissipate her dread of ego-loss: how much self-identity would Emily Dickinson have to cede to ED? It certainly must have been a secret obsession, for she intuited that she was voyaging in uncharted waters quite alien to her family & friends, to say nothing of the local church

64 P-642 ("Me from Myself – to banish"), where ED & Emily Dickinson appear as "mutual Monarch," is the locus classicus recording the struggle within, sometimes a civil war, sometimes an entente cordiale.

people. She says that much deliberation had begun to change fear into a sense of acceptance,

> Because that fearing it so long
> Had almost made it fair –

in the second stanza she gives her fear stronger names: "Dismay," & "Dread." She uses a dressmaker's term here, "Fitting," which makes one think of the famous white dress. And strangely, it evokes the opening lines of P-1109:

> I fit for them –
> I seek the Dark
> Till I am thorough fit.

ED/Emily Dickinson was/were facing a transvaluation of values, taking on a new identity, & learning to submit – but not without misgivings:

> There is a Fitting – a Dismay –
> A Fitting – a Despair –
> 'Tis harder knowing it is Due
> Than knowing it is Here.

It is as has been said of death: the torturous anticipation is much worse than the event itself which, on the deathbed, may produce unexpected consent.

The third stanza confirms the "Fitting," the "Trying on": ED recalls "Trying on the Utmost." "Utmost" means "the greatest degree of consciousness," Buddha Mind.

This poem *evolves,* in the way ED's own consciousness evolved: the fear became Dismay, became Despair, became Terribler. The morning she first donned her white dress, she fully committed herself to her transformation into ED. The dress was her outward sign of a commitment to the rest of her life as ED, "A whole existence through."

1684

The Blunder is in estimate.
Eternity is there
We say, as of a Station –
Meanwhile he is so near
He joins me in my Ramble –
Divides abode with me –
No Friend have I that so persists
As this Eternity.

RAMBLING WITH ETERNITY

ED thinks of ego-transcendence (Eternity) as her welcome guest, as in P-674, "The Soul that hath a Guest." It is also her mysterious friend, as in P-679:

> Conscious am I in my Chamber,
> Of a shapeless friend –

Of this friend she says in the present poem,

> No Friend have I that so persists
> As this Eternity.

"To persist" implies continuance in clock time – which is exactly what ED experienced throughout her life: episodes of Eternal Now "persisted," nor would they be denied (Random House Dictionary says of "to persist," "to continue firmly in spite of opposition").

When ED speaks of "Eternity" as persisting in her own life, she recognizes the need to define it, so as not to be misunderstood by an egocentric reader. The conventional reader thinks of eternity as a "long time," "unending years," "eons" (cf. the expression "forever & a day"). This colloquial meaning is a "Blunder," or egregious mistake, because Enlightenment reveals Eternity to be Now, the Eternal Now.[65] Egocentrically we think of eternity as

65 Interestingly "blunder" comes from Old Norse ***blunda***, "shut one's eyes." Egocentric people are commonly regarded by transcendentalists as going through life with their eyes closed.

a continuum, a time line. Conventional church people think of eternity as Heaven, a place you "go to" when you die – a railway terminus, as it were, or "Station," as ED says in line 3.

"Ramble" (line 5) means to walk, talk, or write aimlessly, which is to say live one's life without ego-intentions. This is ED's way of realizing the Noble Eightfold Path, with "right" thought, speech, action, etc. led by non-ego intuition. To ramble with pencil on paper evokes the practice of automatic writing, akin to ED's alertness to the "unsummoned" word (P-1126), the inspiration from beyond the limits of ego. Unconditioned awareness is her roommate as it were, who "divides abode" with her.

815

The Luxury to apprehend
The Luxury 'twould be
To look at Thee a single time
An Epicure of Me

In whatsoever Presence makes
Till for a further Food
I scarcely recollect to starve
So first am I supplied –

The Luxury to meditate
The Luxury it was
To banquet on thy Countenance
A Sumptuousness bestows

On plainer Days, whose Table far
As Certainty can see
Is laden with a single Crumb
The Consciousness of Thee.

THE LUXURY TO MEDITATE

ED addresses Buddha Mind with many different honorifics – "Sire," "Lord," "Master," "Jupiter," "Majesty," etc. – because to a grateful awakened consciousness the awakening itself appears as a Saving Presence, a "savior." It seems to have saved one from the lifelong folly of superstitious attachment to the ego-identity. In the present poem she calls Buddha Mind an "Epicure" of herself. This metaphor most likely springs from her understanding of the philosophy of Epicurus, which has a good deal in common with the transcendentalist experience.

An epicure is commonly regarded as a person with a taste for luxury, as indicated in the first stanza – but ED has other things in mind, naturally. Epicurus taught that we live in a material universe unregulated by divine providence. While the transcendentalists are by no means "materialists," in the sense of rejecting idealism, they are empiricists accepting only their own, personal experience of the material world, their basic source of data. Even though ED, like other Western transcendentalists, often used Christian vocabulary to describe her experience, in the long run she, like Epicurus, did not accept the notion of a divine providence – God – regulating the universe, much less interfering in the affairs of men & women.

Epicurus was a "long-term" hedonist, not a "short-term" hedonist. "Hedonism" generally refers to the latter – "Eat, drink & be merry," ***carpe diem***, etc. – but Epicurus, like the transcendentalists, prized spiritual pleasure above all, & – especially – freedom from fear & suffering. I say "especially," because this idea echoes the Buddhist experience of freedom from the suffering of ego-attachments. Ego-transcendence is an incredible release from ego-suffering.

If you experience enlightenment you immediately recognize that this state of mind is who you really are. It is your deeper Self. This is Buddha Mind, awakened mind, revealing you to yourself. ED calls it an "Epicure" of who she is, which is a very neat way of putting it.

In the second stanza ED makes the epicurean point that spiritual food has a significance far beyond that of table food. It bestows an abundance [L. *luxus*], or "sumptuousness" [Line 12 – cf. the "sumptuous moment" of P-1125, & the "sumptuous solitude" of P-1495]. At the same time she implies that she herself is an epicure, one who values the "Luxury to meditate" [line 9]. This makes her the epicure of her Epicure.

"The Luxury to meditate" is a feeling commonly recognized by actual meditators. They experience the greatest spiritual abundance in life as the result of their practice. Daily meditation over the years is not only a rich experience in itself; it enriches every aspect of life.

ED was always meditating, not formally, but in the way she went about living daily life, especially in the many hours she spent alone, gardening. When she experienced Unity with Nature, she "banqueted" on its "Countenance," the "look" of Buddha Mind [stanza three]. Without this Unity, the days are "plainer" [last stanza], "laden with a single Crumb" – recollection of Buddha Mind, the Unity that seems to "come & go." We have already seen this paradox addressed in P-1309:

The Infinite a sudden Guest
Has been assumed to be –
But how can that stupendous come
Which never went away?

Experience of Unity is a banquet; recollection of Unity is a Crumb. This is akin to the "Crumb" of P-791 ("God gave a Loaf to every Bird"), meaning a small but real access to instinctual, non-ego mind.

745

Renunciation – is a piercing Virtue –
The letting go
A Presence – for an Expectation –
Not now –
The putting out of Eyes –
Just Sunrise –
Lest Day –
Day's Great Progenitor –
Outvie
Renunciation – is the Choosing
Against itself –
Itself to justify
Unto itself –
When larger function –
Make that appear –
Smaller – that Covered Vision – Here –

No Rack can torture me –
My Soul – at Liberty –
Behind this mortal Bone
There knits a bolder One –

(P-384, first stanza)

RENUNCIATION

In this poem about renunciation ED does not explain what it is that is being renounced. The question can be answered in two different ways – egocentrically, or transcendentally. Richard Sewall, in his biography of Dickinson, offers the egocentric explanation: Dickinson was renouncing social commitment, by contrast to her father & her brother, who "overcommited" themselves.[66] Dickinson needed to keep her creative life alive by making the necessary time & place for it, an attitude famously exemplified by Virginia Woolf: a creative woman needs a time & place of her own.

Sewall's explanation, like most egocentric accounts of Dickinson's ways, makes perfect sense, & is surely on target. What bothers me, however, is the question of whether ED would make that kind of renunciation the primary subject of a poem. ED is certainly "choosing against herself," as Sewall points out; but I think she was choosing against herself in a more basic, existentialist way, the transcendentalist way. ED was choosing herself over Emily Dickinson as the dominant voice of Psyche.

66 See Sewall, *The Life of Emily Dickinson*, 656-657.

She was renouncing the ego-identity as the basic reality of her life. This was a "piercing Virtue."

This "piercing Virtue" is the raison d'être of the so-called renunciate societies (monastic orders) whose members gain merit for honoring their vows. Renouncing the value-system of the ego-self is, of course, a theme universal to Buddhist meditators. American Buddhists in particular face the daunting task of transcending a powerful, dominant Western ego. Typically, the American Buddhist begins by renouncing the usual, everyday ego priorities in order to set aside time for the practice. You get a zafu (meditator's cushion), put it in a special space, & require yourself to sit there alone, for longer & longer periods of time. This is not easy for a busy young American immersed in the stresses of the American Way of Life; it requires a serious struggle with the clamorous ego-self.

As a natural-born transcendentalist ED already had discovered her treasure, her enlightenment; what she needed to renounce was not only social priorities, but also the feeling that her daily identity as "Emily Dickinson" defined who she was. This renunciation is a ***piercing*** Virtue, because, as a form of "tough love," it requires you to reject the bondage of social intercourse as a sop to needy ego. Friends prop each other up by mutually confirming the ego-reality.

But this renunciation is also a piercing ***Virtue,*** because it remains loyal to a truth alien to one's familiars. Ego is a large Presence (line 3) in Psyche, which you let go for an "Expectation."

This is a basic theme in Buddha individuation, which, as noted above, distinguishes between Realization & Actualization – satori on the one hand, & on the other, the gradual creation of an everyday transcendent awareness. Those who evolve in this way are easily recognized by their serene charisma. They are Awake all day long, every day.

ED certainly would have been aware of this issue. One does

not spend life taking ego seriously, while enjoying intermittent vacations of ego-transcendence. Enlightenment raises the "Expectation" that one will continue to individuate more & more in the direction of non-ego; one's existential course has been set.

P-327 begins this way:

> Before I got my eye put out
> I like as well to see –
> As other Creatures, that have Eyes
> And know no other way –

In the present poem this image recurs in line 5, "The putting out of Eyes." "Sunrise" – "*Just* Sunrise" – is the initial experience. But the day that follows sunrise still belongs to the ego-identity, & may easily "outvie / Renunciation" (9-10). "Just Sunrise" is the choosing against itself, ED's choosing against Emily Dickinson. The Sunrise makes apparent the "larger function" (14), what ED called the Eternal Function in P-856.

"Vision" (last line) is the "act of seeing," before you got your eye put out. So this poem is not simply about Emily Dickinson deciding to socialize less; it's about ED recognizing that her priorities outvie those of Emily Dickinson.

936

This Dust, and its Feature –
Accredited – Today –
Will in a second Future –
Cease to identify –

This Mind, and its measure –
A too minute Area
For its enlarged inspection's
Comparison – appear –

This World, and its species
A too concluded show
For its absorbed Attention's
Remotest scrutiny –

MEDITATION: THE SCRUTINY OF ABSORBED ATTENTION

Ed regularly uses "dust" in the sense of "human being," just as the Christians ("dust to dust").[67] In the present poem she says that when we are conceived, the dust becomes "accredited," with human features, & so "identifies" us. At death this dust is scattered &

> Will in a second Future –
> Cease to identify –

The mind, as a physical brain, however – "This Mind, and its measure" – appears to offer "A too minute Area" for an "enlarged inspection" (inspecting the brain as Mind). The brain, as part of the body, is also dust – but as Mind, "The Brain – is wider than the Sky" (P-632).

This World & all within it – its species – is both Dust & Mind. When we, as human beings, think about the World Reality, this is the World's "absorbed Attention," since Mind is World. One cannot perform the "Remotest scrutiny" – the most remote, the highest or deepest scrutiny – because This World is "A too concluded show."

How can anything be "too concluded"? It can't, in the usual sense of the word, but here I take "concluded" to mean "closed," in the sense of "closed to scrutiny." When the Mind-as-World attempts to scrutinize itself with "absorbed attention," the outward "show" disappears.

---

67 See especially poems 491, 813, 976, 1384, & 1630.

"Absorbed Attention" naturally evokes the idea of formal meditation, wherein we give our focused awareness to the Mind itself as the World Reality liberated from all ego-clutter. Our remotest scrutiny is at the farthest remove from ego-attention: this was the focus of ED's "absorbed attention" to the World-as-Nature.

ED knew a thing or two about "absorbed attention" which, in the transcendentalist sense, means meditation in the most general form, as Buddhist *dhyana* (Skt., "absorption, meditation"). *Dhyana*

> refers not so much to the formal practice of meditation but to the meditative nature of all experience, an unmoving quality that transcends goal-oriented activity and that exudes compassion that does not depend on results.[68]

In this sense ED's life & poetry are a single *dhyana*. It is not goal-oriented, not interested in results, & is rooted in compassion as bodhicitta, "awakened heart." In the present poem ED says that the inner mystery of Nature's "show" finally eludes the farthest reach of her absorbed attention; nevertheless, the "accredited Dust" that identifies her has, as its primary feature, ED's absorbed attention concerning the nature of Nature. It was her Main Chance, & she was devoted to making the most of it. I think of this whenever I give ED the scrutiny of my own kind of absorbed attention.

---

68 Barry Boyce, in *Shambhala Sun*, (March, 05), 51. Skt. *dhyana*, Chin. *ch'an*, & Jap. *zen* are cognates.

540

I took my Power in my Hand –
And went against the World –
'Twas not so much as David – had –
But I – was twice as bold –

I aimed my Pebble – but Myself
Was all the one that fell –
Was it Goliah – was too large –
Or was it myself – too small?

EGO, CHAMPION OF THE PHILISTINES: THE DIFFICULT PATH

The story of David & Goliath appears in 1 Sam.17. It is significant, I think, that even though Goliath, the champion of the Philistines, is named twice (17: 4, 23), he is repeatedly referred to as "the Philistine" (21 times – twice as the "uncircumcised Philistine").

When ED sees herself as going "against the World," this is the world of the Philistines – commonplace, materialistic people – & ego is their champion. This is both the collective ego of the community, & her own ego-self, reared to be an integral part of her community.

ED says that for a weapon she had "not so much as David had." She had her poetic voice as Witness/Poet, & so "I took my Power in my Hand."

Keeping in mind that Goliath is both the collective ego & ED's own social identity, we understand why she says

> I aimed my Pebble – but Myself
> Was all the one that fell –

This entails a nice paradox, since both David & Goliath represent the two different identities sharing one consciousness: ED & Emily Dickinson, the "Mutual Monarch(s)" of P-642, where she complains, "But since Myself – assault Me - / How have I peace…?"

It is probably significant that ED writes "Myself" (capitalized, line 5), & "myself" (lower case, line 8), suggesting the Higher Self & the everyday ego-self. Speaking as Emily Dickinson, she sees the Higher Self as having fallen, because the power of ego is (1) too mighty a Goliath, & (2) too small a David. To me this is a seductive example of ED's intellectual love of paradox.

The conflict of which she speaks is well known to all serious meditators. The American Buddhist publications[69] regularly address the issue – namely, the fact that ego is both too large & too small for the enterprise of ego-transcendence. Ego is too large to be defeated very easily, even by the most arduous & persistent practice of meditation; at the same time, ego is also too small – too small-minded – to surrender its monopoly of Psyche, to surrender it permanently to the Higher Self. This is especially true of American Buddhists.

In the present poem ED recognizes that in the current stage of her spiritual development it was the Higher Self that "fell." Buddhist practitioners repeatedly strive to defeat the Goliath of the ego-self, & repeatedly find that this very Goliath is "too small" to submit. This story is all too common among the American Buddhists. With the best will & determination they spend years devoted to their practice, but seem unable to achieve the uncanny detachment of the Asian masters who have come to teach them. For Buddhism, the American ego seems to be the Final Frontier.

69 *Tricycle, Shambhala Sun, Buddhadharma.*

1592

The Lassitudes of Contemplation
Beget a force
They are the spirit's still vacation
That him refresh –
The Dreams consolidate in action –
What mettle fair

CONTEMPLATING, MEDITATING

ED begins this poem by alluding to the state of mind traditionally associated with formal meditation: "The Lassitudes of Contemplation." I take "lassitude" to mean not "weariness," but rather "soft indifference." "Weariness" is not the indicated meaning, because ED says that these lassitudes "Beget a force."

"Lassitudes," in the plural, evokes the steady, soft indifference to the stream of ego-concerns that bombard the mind during meditation – what Buddhists call "monkey-mind." The Buddhist adept Bhante Henepola Gunaratana, in his book ***Mindfulness in Plain English,*** discusses this phenomenon in the context of vipassana ("insight") meditation, where one learns to move from "thinking'" to "observing":

> When you first begin this procedure, expect to face some difficulties. Your mind will wander off constantly, darting around like a bumblebee and zooming off on wild tangents. Try not to worry. The monkey-mind phenomenon is well known. It is something that every advanced meditator has had to deal with.[70]

With a steady indifference to ego-concerns the mind becomes ***vacated,*** or still, what ED here calls "the spirit's still vacation," an emptying of the mind. These persistent moments of indifference beget a force that refreshes the spirit. "Dreams" – active, non-ego states of awareness – consolidate in action, the "action" here reflecting ED's naturally ardent temperament ("mettle") to create

70 Quoted in ***Shambhala Sun,*** (September, 2002), 87.

poetry. In fact, in this poem she describes the necessary grounds for her inspiration. In her younger days as Emily Dickinson she led a busy, engaged, everyday life; with the passage of time this tapered off as she became more & more absorbed into her Lassitudes of Contemplation, freeing her from the never-ending ego-demands that most of us live with day in & day out. As the mind of Emily Dickinson became more & more transformed into the mind of ED, her stillness of spirit came to manifest the "still indifference" that we observe in all Buddha images: indifference to infantile ego's cries for attention.

1527

Oh give it Motion – deck it sweet
With Artery and Vein –
Upon its fastened Lips lay words –
Affiance it again
To that Pink stranger we call Dust –
Acquainted more with that
Than with this horizontal one
That will not lift its Hat –

AFFIANCE IT AGAIN!

It begins like a spirited song:

> Oh give it Motion – deck it sweet
> With Artery and Vein –

In this poem ED develops a dialectic between "it" – Buddha Mind – & "this horizontal one" – the ego-identity. Before socialization of the child begins in earnest, consciousness is "affianced" to one's instinctual nature. In traditional tribal societies this "engagement" leads to a marriage, celebrated by age-old rites of passage that confer a transcendent name (as with the Native Americans).

In "civilized" societies, however, formation of the ego-identity splits consciousness off from Psyche, breaking the engagement, so to speak. Nevertheless, every human being carries within the potential to reaffirm, or renew, that early broken engagement. So it happened with ED. Enlightenment "gave Motion" – Vitality – to her heart, her instinctual nature, & suddenly her "fastened Lips" learned to speak as a poet.

For the alienated ego, one's body is a "Pink stranger we call Dust." Theologians & moral philosophers, if egocentric, disparage the human organism as "mere" Dust; ashes to ashes, dust to dust, & all the rest of it. (In P-813, one of her great cemetery poems, ED reverses that point of view, & asks us to consider that "This quiet Dust was Gentlemen and Ladies / And Lads and Girls.")

Enlightenment "acquaints" one anew with the body, living & breathing *spiritus*; it *centers* one. It soars aloft, as an eagle. (In P-690 ED says that ego partakes of life as robins pecking at crumbs, because "The Eagle's Golden Breakfast strangles – Them." Awakening is Dawn, so naturally your first meal is a Golden Breakfast.)

Ego-transcendence, then, is experienced as a soaring upward. The ego-identity is a horizontal one that will not "lift its hat," i.e., will not even acknowledge the existence of Buddha Mind. How could it?

CEMETERY MEDITATION

1147

After a hundred years
Nobody knows the Place
Agony that enacted there
Motionless as Peace

Weeds triumphant ranged
Strangers strolled and spelled
At the lone Orthography
Of the Elder Dead

Winds of Summer Fields
Recollect the way –
Instinct picking up the Key
Dropped by memory –

THE SPIRIT RECOLLECTS THE WAY

Charnel-ground (cemetery) meditation is an ancient Buddhist/ Hindu tradition that consists in meditating, in the presence of death, on the impermanence of life. It also entails meditating on the ego-identity as an empty illusion of reality.

ED's cemetery poetry is an extension of her sense of the egoless Self, since the necropolis is "inhabited" by lost egos – egos that once experienced daily life, only to pass away as if they had never existed at all (which they hadn't!).

For the transcendentalist, then, the cemetery may be experienced as an outward symbol or display of one's own evolving Self. Day after day one is aware of the ego-reality; each episode of ego-transcendence means a new ego-death, as one awakens in the vibrant, egoless Eternal Now. This Eternal Now is the "full void" of which the Buddhists speak. It is void of the ego-identity, & therefore overflowing with the élan vital. (This is a far cry from what egocentric Westerners think "nirvana" means).

In the present poem ED roams an abandoned cemetery, & experiences it as an outer dramatization of the transcendent Self. It is a "no-place," a "not-self," a piece of earth that has reverted to its natural state, overrun by wild growth. Call it Mother Nature's Zen garden.

This is a burial ground long forgotten as such, & no longer tended to. Such is the transcendent Self that has reverted to its original state of nature where the

> Winds of Summer Fields
> Recollect the way

Ironically it is in these "dead & forgotten" surroundings that Instinct – Mother Nature – picks up the Key to Life, "Dropped by memory." Memory is the key to a well-tended cemetery. An abandoned cemetery has been forgotten; it is beyond the memory of the living. The disappeared egos cease to be remembered, just as in the year-to-year life of the transcendentalist. My five-year-old ego has long since disappeared; so has my teenage ego; so has this morning's ego. This ongoing, impermanent ego-self is an abandoned cemetery, overgrown with weeds, reclaimed by Nature. (People attached to their past are keeping a well-tended cemetery.) As all those past egos vanish into limbo, Instinct picks up the Key to life & opens new doors.

496

As far from pity, as complaint –
As cool to speech – as stone –
As numb to Revelation
As if my Trade were Bone –

As far from Time – as History –
As near yourself – Today –
As Children, to the Rainbow's scarf –
Or Sunset's Yellow play

To eyelids in the Sepulchre –
How dumb the Dancer Lies –
While Color's Revelations break –
And blaze – the Butterflies!

HOW DUMB, HOW NUMB

Cemetery meditation comes naturally to ED, & has an important place in her view of ego & impermanence. To the transcendentalist, the ego-self is a transient phenomenon that keeps dying, like the good citizens of Amherst. Each episode of ego-transcendence means another ego-death, after which ego is reborn (cf. P-280, "I felt a funeral in my brain").

In the present poem ED is meditating in the graveyard. In the first stanza she leads us to believe that she is describing the dearly departed,

> As far from pity, as complaint –
> As cool to speech – as stone –
> As numb to Revelation

but then says that she is talking about herself: "As if my Trade were Bone."

It is true that the dead are as far from the warmth of daily life as pity is from complaint – the distance between compassion & no-compassion.

It is also true that the dead are stonily dead to human speech, just as ED, the one who experiences enlightenment as ineffable. (ED leaves speech up to Emily Dickinson.) But how can ED be "numb to Revelation"? Isn't enlightenment itself a Revelation?

The answer is yes – the first time it occurs. After that, it becomes "nothing special," as Zen teachers say. You come to accept naturally the Way of Reality. If you dwell in the Tao, like the cat or the rat, the Tao is nothing special. Dharma is dharma, adjective-free.

In a Christian burial ground "Revelation" takes on a Christian meaning. Christianity itself is a "revealed religion." ED does not believe in the Resurrection, especially the Resurrection of the ego-identity! (See P-215, for example, "What is – 'Paradise'".) ED is as "numb to Revelation" as the corpses & skeletons buried all around her. It is, she says, as if her "Trade were Bone."

The Buddhist or Hindu charnel meditator takes up the "Trade of Bone(s)." This becomes his daily occupation, & "Trade of Bone" is an arresting ED coinage.

In the Eternal Now "you" are "As far from Time – as History." Past clock time is dead, & current clock time is just as dead. In the Eternal Now one experiences the boundless not-self (as Buddhists call it). Like small children awed by a rainbow, one is at One with Nature.

The unawakened self sees not, like closed "eyelids in the Sepulchre." The Dancer – Shiva, Lord of the Cosmic Dance – lies buried in the dumb ignorance of the ego-self. Line 10, "How dumb the Dancer lies," recalls ED's remark in P-272; there she says of ego's repression of the Spirit, "How numb, the Bellows feels!"

Meanwhile the awakening entails "Revelations" quite other than those described in the Christian Bible. No matter how often ego-transcendence occurs, the blaze of butterflies never ceases to be sensory revelation. The sudden onset of unconditioned awareness is always "something special."

1443

A chilly Peace infests the Grass
The Sun respectful lies –
Not any Trance of industry
These shadows scrutinize –
Whose Allies go no more astray
For service or for Glee –
But all mankind deliver here
From whatsoever sea –

THE IMPERMANENCE OF A BUSY LIFE

"To infest" means to "overrun in large numbers"; so when ED, in this cemetery poem, says that "A chilly Peace infests the Grass," she is alluding to the large number of "dead people" around her, who lie buried in "chilly Peace." At sunset the sun itself begins to "lie down," as if weary after a hard day's work, much as in the "Pastoral" made famous by Benjamin Britten, which begins:

> The day's grown old; the fainting sun
> Has but a little way to run,
> And yet his steeds, with all his skill,
> Scarce lug the chariot down the hill.[71]

(This image is evoked in P-1636: "The Sun is reining to the West...")

At this time of day the deepening shadows do not "scrutinize" (reveal, allow us to scrutinize) any sign of activity.

"Trance of industry," says ED, which is one of her typically complex word choices. [72] "Industry" means "busyness, industrious activity," & its association here with "Trance" produces an unexpected chemistry. "Trance" usually evokes the idea of a medium (as at a séance) in a half-conscious state, deeply absorbed in connecting with the Other Side; whereas the transcendentalist (like the Buddhists adepts) regards conventional, everyday ego-activity as a trance from which it is possible to awaken, i.e. to

71 "Serenade for Tenor, Horn, and Strings."

72 See P-1126, "shall I take thee, the Poet says," where ED describes the process of choosing *le mot juste.*

become enlightened, or fully awake to the dharma. Such is the meaning of Buddha Mind.

In the present poem the "dead people" show no "Trance of industry." Each ego-self has died to the world & has vanished into the dharma. These former ego-selves no longer enjoy as "Allies" the shadows that dogged their footsteps where they were industriously living in the trance of their brief incarnation.

Each of them kept busy, now rendering service, now seeking Glee, or entertainment [line 6]. In the end, the shadows deliver us all "From whatsoever sea." Abruptly. Just like that.

We never know we go when we are going –
We jest and shut the Door –
Fate – following – behind us bolts it –
And we accost no more –

(P-1523)

1221

Some we see no more, Tenements of Wonder
Occupy to us though perhaps to them
Simpler are the Days than the Supposition
Their removing Manners
Leave us to presume

That oblique Belief which we call Conjecture
Grapples with a Theme stubborn as Sublime
Able as the Dust to equip its feature
Adequate as Drums
To enlist the Tomb.

DUST TO DUST

We think of the tenement as an overcrowded building divided into separate rooms, & situated in a district distinct from the rest of the city. All of this, as a complex metaphor, applies to our cemeteries: "Tenements of Wonder," as ED calls them here – "wonder," in the sense of "conjecture."

The first two lines say (if we recast the fluid syntax), "Some, whom we see no more, occupy what to us are Tenements of Wonder, though perhaps to them..."

"...perhaps to them (she goes on to say) "their days are simpler than their everyday personalities (Manners) leave us to presume." I take "remove" (as in "Their removing Manners") in its earlier sense. "to move from one place to another."

The Christian idea of an afterlife presumes that the ego-identity (personality) will survive death in the form of a soul either in heaven or in hell. This belief is satirized in P-215:

> What is - "Paradise" –
> Who live there –
> Are they "Farmers" –
> Do they "hoe" –
> Do they know that this is "Amherst" –
> And that I – am coming – too –

For ED, as a transcendentalist, the "blind faith" demanded by theology is an "oblique Belief" (line 6), being indirect, mediated, & not based on empirical experience. Anyone may experience the grace of satori, but all theological interpretation of satori is conjecture. If one gives satori any such "theme," then it is "Able as the Dust to equip its feature."

For ED "dust" is a metaphor for the physical human being, as in P-813:

> This quiet Dust was Gentlemen and Ladies
> And Lads and Girls –
> Was laughter and ability and Sighing
> And Frocks and Curls.

When we die, it is "dust to dust," meaning that at the beginning of each life the Dust comes together to "equip its feature," & at the end it again disperses. Religious belief does the same: with the birth of each member of society the local belief "equips its feature": it is "Sublime," & it is also "stubborn." ED herself was especially aware of this stubbornness, since friends & family early pressured her to join the church.

But religious belief also disperses like dust at the end. It "enlists" the Tomb, engages it in its service, as do the drums beating a dirge. As a matter of fact, Christian teaching seems to be a dirge commemorating death as the threshold to reward or punishment, especially in the fire-&-brimstone preaching popular among the preachers of the tent revival meetings customary in ED's day.

457

Sweet – safe – Houses –
Glad – gay – Houses –
Sealed so stately tight –
Lids of Steel – on Lids of Marble –
Locking Bare feet out –

Brooks of Plush – in Banks of Satin
Not so softly fall
As the laughter – and the whisper –
From their People Pearl –

No Bald Death – affront their Parlors –
No Bold Sickness come
To deface their Stately Treasures –
Anguish – and the Tomb –

Hum by – in Muffled Coaches –
Lest they – wonder Why –
Any – for the Press of Smiling –
Interrupt – to die –

NECROPOLIS

ED regularly regards the cemetery as a necropolis, a "city of the dead." The term is paradoxical, since it suggests that the inhabitants are "dead people," i.e., persons yet, not decaying matter.[73]

For a transcendentalist the cemetery proclaims the unreality of the ego-identity which, throughout one's lifetime is already a ghostly presence. If you have experienced ego-transcendence, you know that ego is an illusion; the ego has "died" – but it will come back as a ghost in your everyday life. ED coexisted with her friendly ghost, Emily Dickinson.

The poignancy of ED's cemetery poems lies in the fact that she & Emily Dickinson visit the cemetery together, to meditate on the ghosts. Both ED & Emily Dickinson feel deep compassion for them. They lived a short while, loving & suffering, & for ED, the local cemetery is "Our Town." These ghosts cannot hang on to their fading identity, so ED lends a hand, as we have seen, in P-813, "This quiet Dust was Gentlemen and Ladies..."

ED regards these graves as lovely houses, tightly sealed. This is not to prevent entry, it is to prevent exit. And if you visit these houses, there is a protocol: these graves enforce a dress code. You cannot enter barefoot! This is a fine piece of mellow irony. In P-340, about foot & boot ("Is Bliss, then, such Abyss") ED sees the shoe as the ego-identity, & the bare foot as the true self. (There she notes Emily Dickinson's attachment to the boot).

For "Pearl" (line 9), read "Purl," meaning "to flow with a

73 Peter S. Beagle's novel, ***A Fine and Quiet Place,*** is a classic of cemetery literature in this vein.

murmuring sound." In the cemetery ED detects a quiet, ghostly murmur arising from all these faded ego-identities. This includes Emily Dickinson, whose ghostly murmur strives to maintain her hold on life in Amherst (eventually she turns her vitality over to ED).

Cemeteries are regularly visited by funeral processions, of course – "muffled" (line 4). Why "muffled"? More mellow irony here: funeral processions must not awaken the "dead people" already here, lest they wonder why anybody would interrupt the ego-optimism in the face of impermanence.

When ED experienced ego-transcendence she recognized that she had interrupted Emily Dickinson's upbeat self, in order to let it die. Now the question becomes, do you want to exorcise the ghost, or do you want to nourish it? Do you believe that the dead should bury the dead, or do you believe that the ghosts should be honored? ED honored the ghost of Emily Dickinson, because it let her become ED.

ED calls graves "safe – Houses" (line 1), which evokes our modern use of the term, "safe house," meaning (1) a place of refuge, & (2) a place for clandestine activities. The "dead people" residing in the cemetery have found their refuge, & as ghosts are free to conduct their clandestine activities (such as haunting the poetry of ED).

1674

Not any sunny tone
From any fervent zone
Find entrance there –
Better a grave of Balm
Toward human nature's home –
And Robins near –
Than a stupendous Tomb
Proclaiming to the Gloom
How dead we are –

211

Come slowly – Eden!
Lips unused to Thee –
Bashful – sip thy Jessamines –
As the fainting Bee –

Reaching late his flower,
Round her chamber hums –
Counts his nectars –
Enters – and is lost in Balms.

EGO-LOSS, TEMPORARY & PERMANENT

For ED the cemetery is a Necropolis of egos dead for good. Like any other transcendentalist, she lives daily aware of the ego-identity as a phenomenon that comes & goes fitfully. In the ego-dominant mode one's ego-identity seems palpably ***real;*** with ego-transcendence it is annihilated, & one comes alive in the balm of oceanic consciousness. "Balm" is part of ED's transcendentalist vocabulary, & it is interesting to me that my Random House Dictionary defines "balm" as "anything that heals, soothes, or mitigates pain." This definition actually sums up the meaning the Buddha's Four Noble Truths: life is pain caused by ego-attachment, & this pain is mitigated by ego-transcendence.

P-211 is coupled with P-1674 here because of ED's reference to the Balm of Eden. The "fainting Bee" evokes the ego-awareness that swoons, "lost in Balms." This is "human nature's home" (line 5 of P-1674).

Eden belongs to the "pre-ego" state of awareness, which may be later revisited as "non-ego." In P-211 ED wants to savor the experience: "Come slowly – Eden!" She feels "Bashful," or "timid," as she says in P-1335:

> Not when we know, the Power accosts –
> The Garment of Surprise
> Was all our timid Mother wore
> At Home – in Paradise.

Such is the difference between transcendent ego-death & the real thing. One is "human nature's home," & the other is the gloom of a tomb proclaiming how dead ego is, was, & always will be; for the last line of P-1674 refers to ego – whether in the Necropolis or here in the everyday life we call reality.

BIBLIOGRAPHY

Allen, Rupert C. ***Solitary Prowess: The Transcendentalist Poetry of Emily Dickinson.*** San Francisco: Saru Press, 2005.

-------. ***The Yin–Yang Journal: An Alternative Reading of the Tao Te Ching.*** San Francisco: Saru Press, 1996.

American Heritage, New York: Feb/March, 2005

Antiques Magazine. New York: Sept, 2003

Art & Antiques. New York: May, 2005.

Beagle, Peter S. ***A Fine and Private Place.*** New York: Dell, 1960.

The Best Poems of the English Language. Harold Bloom, ed. New York: Harper Collins, 2004.

Blyth, R.H. ***Haiku.*** 4 vols. Tokyo: Hokuseido Press, 1949-52. Buddhadharma, Boulder, Colorado.

Dickinson, Emily. ***The Complete Poems of Emily Dickinson.*** Thomas H. Johnson, ed. Boston: Little, Brown and Co., 1960

-------. ***Poems.*** John Malcolm Brinnin, ed. New York: Dell, 1960.

-------. ***Poems.*** Brenda Hillman, ed. Boston: Shambhala, 1995.

-------. ***Poems.*** Louis Untermeyer, ed. New York: Heritage Press, 1952.

Habegger, Alfred. ***My Wars Are Laid Away In Books.*** New York: Modern Library, 2002.

Hagen, Steve. ***Buddhism Plain and Simple.*** Boston: Charles Tuttle, 1997.

Kapleau, Philip. *The Three Pillars of Zen.* New York: Anchor Books, 1989.

Keown, Damien. *A Dictionary of Buddhism.* New York: Oxford Univ. Press, 2003.

Lao Tzu. *Tao Te Ching.* John C. Wu, tr. New York: St. John's Univ. Press, 1961.

Look Who's Talking: An Anthology of Voices in the Modern American Short Story. Bruce Weber, ed. New York: Washington Square Press, 1986.

Maguire, Jack. *Essential Buddhism.* New York: Pocket Books, 2001.

Nisargadatta, Maharaj. *I Am That.* Bombay: 1973.

Parabola. New York: Summer, 2003.

Sewall, Richard B. *The Life of Emily Dickinson.* Cambridge: Harvard Univ. Press, 1974.

Shambhala Sun. Boulder Colorado.

Shift. Petaluma, CA: March-May, 2004.

Solomon, Deborah. *Utopia Parkway: The Life and Work of Joseph Cornell.* New York: Farrar, Straus and Giroux, 1997.

Stevens, Wallace. *The Necessary Angel.* New York: Alfred Knopf, 1951.

Teachings of Zen. Thomas Cleary, tr. Boston: Shambhala, 1998

Thoreau, Henry David. *Journal.* Vols.7-20 in *The Writings of Henry David Thoreau.* New York: Houghton Mifflin, 1906.

Thurman, Robert. *Infinite Life: Seven Virtues for Living Well.* New York: Riverhead Books, 2004.

Tricycle: The Buddhist Review. New York.

Wolff, Cynthia. *Emily Dickinson.* New York: Knopf, 1986.

INDEX

INDEX OF FIRST LINES

**Asterisk indicates full quotation*

www.ingramcontent.com/pod-product-compliance
Ingram Content Group UK Ltd.
Pitfield, Milton Keynes, MK11 3LW, UK
UKHW020131250726
13967UKWH00002B/597